# PORTRAIT OF A MAN STANDING

SALVADOR DE MADARIAGA

# *Portrait of*
# *a Man Standing*

---

UNIVERSITY OF ALABAMA PRESS

UNIVERSITY, ALABAMA

TO DR JOSEPH TRUETA

*In memory of twenty-five years of Sunday walks
in the countryside of Oxford*

'Some trilobites could see all round; but none above.'
R. L. Gregory, *Eye and Brain*

# PREFACE

It is not without much diffidence that I launch in its English garb this meditation on—everything. To my deep regret, I cannot entertain any illusions about the fact that it is conceived in a spirit far from congenial to the English. When I say 'English' I also have in mind the Americans, as well as the Australians, Canadians, New Zealanders, Scots, and even the Welsh. I should perhaps have written 'Anglo-Saxon'; but I was not able to. Somehow or other, it does not suit. It is one of those awkward misnomers which are in themselves one of the signs of the English way of living—indeed of being.

As an unrepentant Spaniard I am thoroughly alien to the English genius—much as I love to dwell on it with genuine admiration and fascination: to such a degree, indeed, that it has become a commonplace of Spanish contemporary criticism to label me 'anglified'. Well, we all know the ways of critics, so why worry? Were I as anglified as they say, I should not now be so diffident about offering the 'Pan-English' public this odd kind of offspring. The core of my diffidence is no other than this: as I point out in my essay, I consider the English (again *lato sensu*) as the most perfect herd on earth. (No offence, by the way, as the essay will show; on the contrary, an appreciation of a natural gift and disposition.) While this disquisition amounts to a most imperfect plea for—well, certainly not for the herd. Now herds of the human species are most touchy. Am I then not exposing my creature to being kicked on the head by a young calf at its first encounter with the herd?

Were I to try to explain here what this book is a plea for, I should find myself writing it all over again. Leaving aside, however, the plea element in it, by no means the most important, I should like to state that I wrote this essay because I had to. Surely this is the only legitimate reason

11

or motive for writing at all. For years, I have been drawn to the subject or, at any rate, to one aspect of it: *how to spy on God so as to catch here and there a glimpse of what He is after.* When we mortals say, and go on repeating century after century, that God is silent we surely mean no more than that He does not speak any of our languages. But words are not the only form of utterance, nor often the most direct and straight. Every man in his senses, even if untouched by politics and innocent of diplomacy, knows that people had better be judged by their deeds than by their words. Much as we should like to judge God, we are not equipped for such a task; but we might try to understand or adumbrate His intention by watching Him at work. It has always seemed to me that Creation has a way of dropping hints which, caught alive, so to speak, may lighten in us flashes of intuition about the intentions of its Creator. And I suggest to biologists that, by denying themselves the hypothesis of a purposeful Creator—a self-denial to be admired as well as regretted—they make Creation as baffling and inexplicable as *Hamlet* would be without the Prince.

All I suggest, therefore, in the pages that follow, is that we stand before Creation like a visitor to the Louvre who, drinking in through his eyes that mysterious *St. Anne*, wonders, then reflects, then thinks he sees what was in Leonardo's mind when he conceived his meaningful though silent picture. In other words, a theology upside down. Theology starts from the notion of God and, from this all-containing kernel, deduces every possible attribute and aspect of the Lord and of His world. This it does by adjusting God and His Creation to the laws of the human mind, i.e. by forcing God to be human. What else can human science do? Then, events and beings will have to be explained in terms of the principles and theorems established by theology. While our way here would be the very reverse: not from God downwards to events and beings, but from events and beings upwards to God. It would all begin, therefore, by a kind of watching out and looking around for hints, since, assuming the world to be something less crazy than a tale told by an idiot, intelligence and intention are bound to betray themselves through the gray veil of a universal inscrutability. Instead of forcing God and His Creation to be human, we shall thus be trying to discover what in beings and events may turn out to be divine; and so, by sketching the line and movement into which our glimpses will fall naturally and by themselves, guess the elusive shape and motion of the Creator Himself.

# I

A cow on a field of grass is not a bad starting point. Particularly if there is at least one tree about, not too far though, so that the tree and the cow can be taken in at one glance. An upright and a level form. There is here a curious paradox, one of those hints nature drops now and then for man to catch and ponder on, as if nature asked: do you see what I am driving at? The paradox consists in that while the vegetal kingdom is older than the animal, it is on the whole made up of vertical individuals, while the animal kingdom does not produce a truly vertical type until it ceases to be animal and opens out into mankind.

Do you perceive the human prejudice which underlies that whole sentence? It is assumed that the upright form is higher, more evolved than the horizontal or level, simply because it comes at the end of animal evolution; and the fact that it was there all the time in the older vegetal kingdom is tucked in by the way as a kind of paradox. But the fact is that between the two upright forms, the tree and the human animal, the differences are profound.

The tree feeds itself from the lower end upwards and breathes from the upper end downwards. It sheds its waste products from the upper end, down to the earth. The cow— for she must be considered first, before we come to man—the cow feeds herself from the earth at the front, and sheds her waste products from behind, down to the earth. As in the case of the tree, food and waste products come from the same earth, but in the case of the cow they are closer together, and we begin here—we, human beings—to perceive a revulsion at the ways of nature that we have never felt towards the rotten leaves that feed the roots of the tree. Let that feeling of revulsion be stored in our memories for further use. Reproduction in the cow is also relegated to the hind quarters in a higgedly-piggedly intimacy with excretion of waste. We, human beings, also feel sick at this lack of decency and taste on the part of nature.

The animal arrangement is far more mobile than that of the tree. The tree is stuck to its place on the earth by its roots, and the sight of all those powerful tentacles thrust into the earth this way and that suggests a mutual embrace: the earth retains the tree, but doesn't the tree retain the earth in that many-armed embrace? It would seem that when we pass from the vegetal to the animal kingdom, we leave the world of fixity to enter the world of mobility.

So it is. But not as much as it seems. Look at the cow again. Don't you see a chain of necessity passing from the earth up to her mouth and through her body and the anus to the earth again? You may move the cow to another meadow; you may even feed the cow with hay in a city-shed; but that chain, shorter or longer, remains. Stretch it you can. Break it you cannot. It must remain intact, limiting the mobility of the cow to reasonable distances of her natural grass.

Her form reflects her limitations. Her mouth and nostrils hang close to the earth; her eyes do not rise above the level at which they are set by her stature, and more often than not look downwards. Her sense of smell is powerful and her nostrils are active. One of her features sets her apart from the tree or anything vegetal. Roots and branches in the tree grow forward in the direction assigned to them, so that there is no distinction, no difference in rank, between shoots that bore into the earth and those that grow towards the sides or the sky. But in the cow there is the brain with all its sensual protuberances—eyes, ears, tongue, papillae, and nostril cells. This apparatus *orientates* the cow. It enabled us to speak of 'front' and 'back' and 'hind quarters'. A prologue to greater things.

16

These greater things were to come as the quadruped rose on its hind legs and, freeing its forelimbs, developed the hands—the great revolution. The cow tried to become a tree! How significant that the act of a horse rising on its hind legs should be described in some European languages, in Spanish and German, for instance, as 'to tree itself' (*enarbolarse*, *sich bäumen*)! From the day man ceases to rest on his forelimbs and stands upright, civilization begins. His two forelimbs are freed to seek his food elsewhere than at his feet, mixed with his droppings. His eyes are able to rise above the plane in which they are set, and his front–back orientation becomes an up-and-down polarization. From his animal past he imports the prejudice in favour of front-happenings, intake, over back–happenings, dropping of waste. *Above* becomes more awesome than *below*.

Man has become a tree that has packed up its earth and got moving. But the chain that went from the meadow to the meadow along the body of the cow still binds him to the earth. It is ever present in the thoughts of those brave and keen men at Cape Kennedy. Far suppler and subtler, it remains nonetheless as binding as the roots of the tree that knot it up to the earth below.

Below. Above. Key words. The head, level with the tail in the cow, is now at the very top, the highest part of the body; and highness becomes a dignity in itself. (In the course of the centuries 'Your Highness' will be the form of address for the ruler of the people.) *High* and *low* take on a rank that *front* and *back* had not achieved in animals, in whose obscure consciousness they are both level and probably lumped together in a vague feeling of self. Gradually the new vertical being organizes his planes of perception, action, feeling, and bodily function in a series of levels arranged vertically: intuition highest; intellection next; emotion third; vegetative life fourth. And as these levels vaguely correspond to seeing, inhaling, taking in food, breathing, digesting, procreating and excreting, the two sets of functions fall into the same high–low hierarchy. The old repulsion about mixing excretion with procreation remains somewhat attenuated by the raising of the breasts from the level of digestion to the level of emotion.

This change in the structure of the mammal is capital. It brings in a new form of life destined to a huge share in human life. Love begins as the emotional load of the procreating instinct. The raising of the breasts from the abdomen to the chest means their elevation from the level of instincts to that of emotions. This change was essential to ensure the advent of the civilized or collective phase of mankind.

For there were other changes implicit in the upright position that carried with them formidable advances in the development of men yet were fraught with danger for his social achievements. Level, the cow lived in the midst of the herd, in a world of similar beings bathed in an atmosphere of similar necessities at similar times in similar places. Upright, man is led to live a lonely life. Every man for himself.

As he rose on his feet, man's eyes felt liberated from the world below the horizon, and glanced afar. This developed his mind–glance as well and enabled him to combine and build up his observations under the light his intuition provided. Knowledge brought power to him. Power provided him with the possibility of enslaving other animals, including human animals, to the satisfaction of his needs as an ephemeral individual and to the detriment of his and other species.

His new position, moreover, considerably enlarged the scope of his liberty, or in other words, the field for his will. Liberty is a primary need of all animals, as every pigeon keeper or dog owner knows full well. But the chain of need attaches animals closely to the earth they inhabit, and their faculties being few they cannot increase the ambit of movement granted them by nature. Standing on his feet, the human animal soon perceived that henceforth his ambit of movement had increased beyond his dreams. His hands, eyes and intellect were now at the disposal of his will to widen the scope of his liberty. There was nothing he could not do.

This combination of mind and will might have sealed the doom of the species but for the birth of love. On standing, man and woman had to expose to the light of other eyes those sexual parts which in the all-fours position had remained at least discreetly in the shade. Here again we see emerge another, finer, more delicate form of the repulsion felt by the human being towards excretory parts, operations, and discharges. This time it takes the form of pudicity. The sexual organs have remained too low for the feelings of our species: another criticism that man raises against nature. This attitude reveals the strength of the new form of love, the emotion, and, no longer a mere instinct, the affection for the other as distinct from the passive service of the species.

Not only do we feel that the sexual organs are too low in the scale of the spine, too close to all that excretory part which we find disgusting; we also feel that they are ugly. We have raised love so high—up to the level of our eyes, have we raised it: could it go higher than the light in our life?—we have raised love so high that we could have wished to be able to express it in its man-and-woman form by means of less animal organs, by organs removed as far from the lower abdomen as our forehead or our eyes. We resent this insistence of nature in making us descend to the level of the dog and bitch in order to love.

Nature does not care, of course. She is not thinking of us nor of our love, but of the species. And here again we resent her low tricks (note how naturally I say *low*). She has made desire a wellnigh unconquerable force, stronger by far (in most cases) than that will which we have proudly developed on standing up. There we are, caught. And willy nilly, women have to bear the burden of maternity whenever they let themselves go to their love-emotion. We resent this as a low trick of nature, a lack of respect for an upright man endowed with a scale of values, of course vertical, as vertical as his spine.

In our resentment, we push forward (which for us means upward) our evolution of love. We are going to liberate love from sex to such an extent that we love everybody, men and women and children—everybody, why even animals. And this charity is born of the necessity to move away clear from the chain of sexual desire by which nature drags us *down* to the level of dogs and bitches. Thus, a powerful force is created that is going to discipline the mind and the will of the individual and solve the numberless conflicts of liberties between equally ambitious men. This universal love ranks high among man's aspirations—nearly as 'high' as any other in his ambitious soul.

Nearly as *high*, for there is no getting away from the hierarchy of levels along his vertical structure. Exhilarated by the liberty that had freed his mouth from the grass and his nose and eyes from the earth, he has now freed his emotion from his sex. But the freeing of his eyes has led him to an even more exhilarating freedom. He can now separate the work of his brain from his bodily needs. He watches, perceives, and thinks. Behind the things he sees with his eyes he discovers the ideas of these things, which he sees with his brain; and still more fascinating patterns between these ideas, ideas of ideas, a whole world in which the mind is free.

Thus musing, he soon finds that there are two kinds of happenings around him. Things that happen (some of them to him), and things that he causes to happen. Further, these events that he causes to happen may just occur without or despite his deliberate will or may take the external shape he had devised before they happened. Thus he is led to find the difference between *facts* and *acts*—events that determine man and events determined by him. And he feels that the difference between fact and act is that an act has first been an idea.

Then he remembers how elated he was when he discovered that there was an idea behind everything he saw in nature.

Now that he can look upwards, there is no limit to his skyward vision. What he cannot touch, he can see. What he cannot see, he can imagine. Power comes from the sun. Cold shivers from the moon. Lightning and thunder from the clouds. Earthquakes and floods from the earth and its waters. All those happenings, he knows, manifest forces far bigger than those he can wield. There are about, therefore, centres of thought, will, and emotion other and bigger than man. At this point, the gods are born. And since man has got used to measuring things by means of a vertical scale, the good divine principle will be on high, in heaven and the bad divine principle, below, in the bowels of the earth.

The two principles will struggle in man's own being. What a good idea it was to make man so much like a tree. Far more than it would seem at first. For if we look at him carefully we soon discover that man is the synthesis of a cow and a tree, the spirit of a tree in the body of a cow.

This, of course, assumes that we have a good look at the tree. And as we have just spoken of the spirit of a tree, it might be just as well if we emphasized how rich in spirit trees are apt to be. Speaking of national character! Where in the whole creation is there more character than in trees? The sturdy oak and the sensitive birch and the pensive cypress and the opulent chestnut and the inconsolable willow (though there is a less whiny variety, the willow that can take it) and the calm cedar—irate, prim, tousled, sedate, bare, tortured, gesticulating, skeletal, muscular: how many different characters the world of trees can stage—and I haven't said a word about their flowers.

Now these trees, so different in character, are all built on

21

the same pattern. Every tree may be divided into three sections, the roots, the trunk and the branches and foliage. There is a striking likeness between the first and the last. Both roots and branches are plural, formed in successive ramifications, which suggest a certain collectivism. The roots, moreover, plunge into the dark recesses of the earth in which they absorb the solid and liquid food which will enrich the sap, while the branches and leaves also 'collectivize' themselves in mid-air and take in the gaseous food or breath that will complete the work of the roots. Furthermore, when trees stand together, their collective levels will collectivize further, making up vaster multitudes in the luminous air and in the recesses of the earth. This upper collectivity does more than breathe. Through the chlorophyll of its leaves it transmutes the energy of the sun into chemical energy; and this operation is crucial in the life of the tree, and through it, in all life.

In striking contrast with its upper and lower pluralities, the trunk is single. It stands alone and sometimes, if the tree is tall, it will draw to itself all the attention, and claim to be 'the tree', to the neglect and detriment of the roots and the branches, thus reduced to the status of mere adjuncts or annexes. The trunk is the individualistic section of the tree, a well defined, hard, vertical object which makes up a convenient unit and renders it easy to count numbers.

See how similar to man. For man also can be said to be composed of two collectivities and an individualized trunk. *Down below* the instincts, the roots of his being, plunge into the earth this tree had packed in its inside when it got moving. His roots are plural. They ramify far into the blood plasma of his ancestors, his whole people in fact. *Up above* his intuition forms a no less real if no more visible ramification of branches and twigs around his head; a fascinating fact hinted at in many ways, such as the saying of a man that he has 'a twig of madness'. Think of the aura of the saints, of the long hair of pianists, of the mane-and-brow of Beethoven; think of hats—not, of course, of women's hats, that would be too easy—but of the fact that if you get an accountant, a poet, and an army major to buy three identical hats on the same day in the same shop, they will in a week have modelled them into three entirely different shapes, being three trees of different species, each in search of his own foliage.

And, of course, you will remember the most important function of the foliage: the work of the chlorophyll in the leaves, transmuting the energy of the sun into chemical energy. So the foliage of the human tree transmutes the intuitional energy that it receives from the source of all mind–light into mental energy; and persons of highly developed foliage are rich in—well not precisely intellect, but that faculty *above* the intellect which feeds it with light-energy.

These two faculties, the instinct *below*, the intuition *above*, are collective. They transcend the individual and make him communicate with the common sources of life and power that spread *below* and *above* him. The trunk in man, like the trunk in the tree, is the unit, the individual proper. And it is in the trunk that the typically individual faculties develop—the intellect, the will and the emotion—which in their aggregate make up the mind. Thus, the tree may be said to offer an image of the inner or spiritual shape of man, a first prefiguration through the animal kingdom of what was going to be the spearhead of its animal counterpart.

All this fits in perfectly with that discovery man had made a few pages ago: somewhere in the world there must be centres of thought and action other and bigger than man, gods in fact; as well as with his guess that the good, divine principle must reside on high, and the bad, divine principle must lurk in the bowels of the earth. For it is from the high regions of air and light that his 'foliage' receives its inspiration; and from the bowels of the earth (or from the earth in his bowels) that his troubles and passions arise. And it is in his trunk and head that the two forces battle.

Thus his tree-like standing position leads man to associate the solid and liquid food he receives from his roots with earthbound evil forces; while the gaseous food he gets from his foliage is associated with heaven. And this sense or feeling that air is holy and heavenly gives rise to the double meanings of *pneuma*, *spiritus*, *anima*, hovering between the air we breathe and the seed-conveying wind, and the essence of life. How easy from this attitude to the dichotomy of the world between 'spirit' and 'matter' that holds our thought in thrall: spirit, the gaseous food from on high; matter, the solid and liquid food from below, now seen as concepts derived from the tree–ancestry of the human being, from the branches and the roots. How far will they resist the wear and tear of the inner experience of his trunk and above all his head? For the chief fact about man is that his head has a way of boring into things and events with a tool he names thought.

What is he going to do with all that power? He now sees, reasons, and wills. What of it?

There. The cow has moved. She is now on the left of the tree. Shadier there, you know, and the sun is hot. That is what the cow seems to have *thought*. The tree has not moved. Does he think? Who knows? As for his willing, the sturdy limbs that, mastering all obstacles, have penetrated the earth do not suggest any lack of determination. Is there a guiding light? A line clear enough to stand as a frontier between man–life and cow–life, cow–life and tree–life, would be hard to draw. But a general trend?

My cup of tea . . . I had forgotten all about it. Stone cold. After nearly a whole hour left there on the table, no wonder. No wonder? Why, on the contrary. It is a matter to wonder at. Why should heat be dissipated just because time goes by? Aye. Such is nature. Time will level down everything.

*Down*, mind you. And this is no up-and-down, human, vertical, prejudice. The temperature of the cup of tea goes down. The height of the hill, the temperature of the sun, everything. The sea bottom goes up, though. It all means that things tend to level each other up and down towards a uniform height and temperature.

This universal fact might be put in another way. It has, in fact, been put in another way by the scientists who formulated the second law of thermodynamics. Things tend to change from the less likely to the more likely. Nature shuns the odd. Time makes everything like everything else. Of its own, nature does not produce the singular, it does not even preserve it. An object such as that cup of tea, hotter than its surroundings, is soon forced back into the ranks in point of temperature. Given enough time, the mere forces of nature would reduce the cup and the table and the house to a uniform mass of dust.

But wait: Life turns up and events take the opposite course. From the first cells to the human brain, life, instead of descending into the dust, *disintegrating*, rises from complexity to more complexity, ever *integrating*, until it reaches the unique. Life is ever after the unlikely and the singular. No dog is like any other dog. And what could be more unlikely than the Sistine Chapel or the Ninth Symphony?

Matter and spirit, one might be tempted to say. But it is better to resist the temptation, for it leads to the use of words of no certain meaning. Here is a solid table made of oak. Let us ask our brother the scientist: what is it made of? Wood, he answers—what we call 'cellulose'. But, again? Well, cellulose is a compound of carbon, hydrogen, oxygen and nitrogen. And then? Call them all more or less complicated forms of hydrogen, which is an atom composed of a proton and an electron turning around it under mathematical laws. And what is an electron? A charge of electricity, our brother scientist answers. Wait a minute, we break in, wait a minute. 'A charge' you said. Where is the donkey? There is no donkey at all. The electron is a pure charge of electricity borne by nothing.

Exit matter.

But let's keep asking. What is a charge of electricity? A spot of space round which there is an electrical field, i.e. an area in which active forces can be detected by the attractions and repulsions they cause, and which can be represented by mathematical formulae such as the Fourier series. So that an electron is a spot of space round which energy behaves in accordance with mathematics, i.e. with the law of the human mind; which spot, moreover, turns round the proton in accordance with the said mathematics. In conclusion, matter is energy behaving under the laws of the mind. Why then should we not conclude that matter is a form of the spirit?

The old opposition between spirit and matter breaks down. All is spirit. We must seek elsewhere our line dividing physical from vital evolution. Could it be found in the capacity to create patterns? A daisy, a living thing. Ah yes, but have you looked closely at a flake of snow? It is as symmetrical as a daisy, and it can take on many forms, though they all conform to an hexagonal symmetry. There is complexity for you there, and all out of that simplest of all things, water. Simple and yet so pregnant with beautiful forms—the snow flake and the ice crystal and the icicle, and the wave, and the torrent rich in foam, and the numerous family of the clouds, some like sails in the wind or like flights of birds or like castles and battlements or galleons or snow-capped crests or wings of archangels.

Stay. Those visions are not born of water but of your own human imagination. Lifeless matter can fall into patterns but they are ever the same. Prints of the same original for each form of it. And this again applies to trees as well. Their lovely flowers and their beautiful leaves are patterns printed forever in each species. Nor is this entirely untrue of man himself, whose acts are apt to be as true to pattern as the leaves and flowers of the tree—but, and this is weighty, typical no longer of the species but of the individual.

Would thought be the dividing line? There are still people about who think that animals neither think nor feel, though the cow *felt* and *thought* she would be cooler in the shade by the tree. Such people have not observed how observant a dog can be—and how friendly, huffy, proud, stubborn, how capable of drawing conclusions and of reciprocating good or ill feelings, and even of feeling guilty or ashamed. The difference is subtler than that. It is not to be found in the existence or inexistence of the thinking and the feeling processes but in the quality of thought and feeling.

Remember. The once horizontal shape had to adjust itself to a vertical stance. The cow stood up in imitation of the tree. Man's eyes ceased to be limited to the space below the horizon of his belly; his glance was raised as high above his inner earth as his inner earth was now from the outer earth on which his feet were standing. And this upper scope granted to his eyes meant freedom. Man became able to detach his thought from his bodily needs, indeed from his whole person altogether. He became capable of assimilating the intuitions which his foliage won for him in the upper reaches of space.

And remember that the first outcome of this change was that man became able to invent patterns; no longer to reprint them, as does the crab or the chestnut tree. A pattern is an order. Man became a creator of new forms of order. It is sometimes asserted that the difference between man and the higher mammals lies in language, which enabled tradition to develop and therefore allows accumulation of experience. But at the origin, the difference lies in the ability to create patterns of order; for a language *is* a pattern of order, invented by disinterested thought. It is the outcome of the assumption of the vertical position, of the liberation of man's eyes from earth-bound servitude.

His eyes, now free, rose to heaven. The highest of the high. The exalted place from which intuitions come. Was he not now a creator of patterns, of order? It was but natural that he should extrapolate his freedom and creativeness and his power, erecting on the highest spot of his reality the throne of the freest and most powerful Creator. Man thus created the most exalted pattern of all. This Creator created by him assumed all the powers and qualities of man at their highest and best.

Man saw Him as a kind of Marcus Aurelius–Leonardo–Shakespeare–Descartes–Beethoven–St. John of the Cross rolled into one, every human being stressing the aspect for which he was most alive. But the Creator had a way of evading any and every pattern—least of all, perhaps, the Shakespearean model, for does He not revel in the creation of characters, and is He not equally fond of them all. Even so, any and all of these 'great–man' human patterns fall below His stature, for they were all limited, while it was in His nature that He should become the source of all there is, was and will be.

The Creator, once created, had to pursue His own line, and remain true to His own character as conceived by man. The Creator emancipated Himself from His creator. He became, He had to become, a Creator in His own right. He created all things, from the lowest to the highest—all save Himself. Indeed, He created man.

Then the Creator and His creator, now His creature, compared notes. It was a far less smooth confrontation than might have been anticipated. The creature had no idea of the hugeness of the world he had let in upon himself on creating such an all-in Creator. All time, all space, all spirit, all creatures. God had to become a wonder-worker. Not content with seeing in Him the cause of everything in nature, man endowed Him with the power to cause everything He wished outside, above, or against nature. Man surrounded God with a cloud of mysteries.

And yet, he was not satisfied. There he was, after all, vertical and free—an intelligent, mobile tree, his head rich in spiritual foliage. Must he passively bow before the Omniscient? True, sometimes he fancied he was on the eve of knowing everything. But later, the more he advanced, the less, it seemed to him, he knew. In physical matters, hardly had he explained everything by seeing in the atom a universe in miniature, when the atom vanished under his eyes (their power magnified by gadgets) and transfigured itself into a cloud of mathematical mysteries no less opaque than those of medieval theology. If I am to believe that this thick oak table is but a mass of waves of probability only utterable in abstruse equations, I might just as well believe in the Assumption of the Virgin and in the Immaculate Conception. So grumbled the creature in his downcast foliage, disgruntled at the uncompromising silence of his created but emancipated Creator.

Why can't we know more about things? We were content to remain baffled before the mystery of life. That tobacco–virus . . . Haven't we panted with hope when it crystallized in our laboratories? There it was at last, the bridge between mineral and vegetal nature. But we are still as far as ever from knowing how it all began. Those huge molecules of protein, with their complicated patterns of atoms, their double 'spiral staircases' for 'conveying' 'messages' by whom conceived? No. Just as in the case of the atom, the created Creator lurks behind a screen of subtle complexities woven with still subtler complexities, and—laughs?

Frankly, we don't like it at all. And if only what we knew were a little more encouraging . . . But we are baffled by life. The tree and the cow are harmless enough. But the shark and the tiger . . . As we see it, the three realms of life, the sea, the land and the air, live by and on murder. We have built our society on a firm rejection of murder—within our species; and pride ourselves on our humane ways of killing, which we assume to be better—or 'higher'—than those we see in nature (i.e. the divine ones?).

It is all very puzzling. If He has created everything, including ourselves, how can we disagree with His world? As soon as animal life begins, we feel we have to look away in shame and disgust. Nor can we even rest on a sense of being above it all, for horrors do not stop at the gates of mankind; rather do they become more horrible being performed at a 'higher' level from the earth and its grass. We think of the long trail of blood we call History and shudder. We reflect on the sufferings of children, and stand aghast, baffled beyond consolation by the inescapable reproach to God that it arouses in our hearts.

Does He care about human culture? Then why does His scythe cut down Mozart and Schubert in their youth? Why allow a foolish pipe-smoker absentmindedly to destroy in a few minutes a masterpiece that had taken a lifetime of care to create? Does He care about human virtues? Why let the scoundrel flourish and the bully rule? Does He care for human taste? Our taste is often hurt and even outraged by the lack of taste in creation. Even sunsets, often magnificent, can be vulgar. Why should beauty be so rare among human beings, and when occurring, why so ephemeral? Why should the instruments of love be so ugly and why should they be confined to the vilest parts of the body? Why should the Creator play tricks on us such as the spreading of the nets of desire to ensnare women into maternity?

The head being high up in the upright scale of values, we try hard to explain God as a super-rationalist. Why, even the extravagant tailfan of the peacock, even the chatter of the parrot, are at times explained as the allurements of the male. Why they should be present in peacocks and parrots and absent in the heavy-footed ducks and the ridiculous turkey-cocks is an irrational mystery at the core of all that rationalism. Wouldn't it be more rewarding (in point of truth as well as of entertainment) to see the deeds of the Lord in a gay and carefree independence of any rationalism? Fun, sense of humour, caprice, are they not more sensible hints of the power of the deity than strict adherence to logic's chains? What better proof of the existence of God than an eloquent and ludicrous parrot! How much fun must He have had in creating that gorgeously coloured, winged caricature of man. But then we think of the cruelty of the animal and human world and we shudder.

If our mind comes from God, how is it that it cannot discover the truth of God's world; if our will comes from God, how is it that we cannot approve of the behaviour of God's world; if our sensibility comes from God, how is it that we dislike what for us is the bad taste of many a thing in the world? Nor is this all; for if these three negations were consistent, we might at least rest on a kind of upside down view of God's things. There are, however, so many things we know, approve of, and like in God's world—so many truths, acts of grace, and wonderful sunsets—that the mystery thickens. It seems as if God's nature were not merely different from ours but indifferent to ours. His values, His standards, His aims, are not our values, standards and aims. How then could we have created Him or He us?

Faith leaps over this abyss or takes it in its stride. But the abyss is there for all that. Fortunately? Perhaps. For if there were no such abyss, if the values, standards and aims of God were identical with ours, we might be faced with two ways of accounting for it: one, that God being our creature, had no freedom of His own, and as a God without freedom He would die; the other, that we had divined a Creator who would not allow us any freedom, and as creatures without freedom, we should remain on a semi-animal level, sterile forever.

Things as they are suggest that at some time in the evolutionary process God was content to delegate some of

31

His creative powers to man. From the emergence of man, God shares His Creation with His creature. This implies freedom for man, and therefore a complete autonomy from God as regards intellectual, ethical, and esthetic judgments. How can this freedom manifest itself unless it leads now and then to differing from the goings-on in God's world?

This explanation is perhaps as good as can be put forward from the human side. It does not follow that it is God's—which, we must own, is the only one that matters. Even for us, that human explanation leaves unsatisfied our chief cause of concern. What worries us is not so much that we differ from God but that God differs from us. How *could* He make us so different from Himself? In a moment of bitter cynicism, Voltaire wrote: 'God made man in His image; but man has returned the compliment to Him.' This was meant to be sarcastically pessimistic; it turns out to be starry-eyedly optimistic. The trouble is that we differ as much from God as He from us.

One way out might be, at any rate for some, to assume that God has His own explanation, which He cannot reveal to us without its ceasing to be His. The Lord's perspective must be vaster than ours in a degree incommensurably higher than our perspective is vaster than that of a mouse or of a fly. That cow that conceived the ambition of standing upright like a tree and became a man, with his head high above the grass, dreamt of a vastly enlarged man with his head in the blue sky, who would be the Creator of all things. But the blue sky turned out to be a mere veil—and beyond it, infinite space opens its unfathomable halls as the abode of the unfathomable Spirit.

## 2

Standing is not easy for man. He has not yet got used to it, though he has been trying for ages. If he stands for long, his bones ache with the sheer weight of his body; so that tyrants and third-degree experts who wish to break a man's spirit need but keep him standing for a few hours. No better proof could be adduced of the fact that standing is not a natural position for man. Chairs and beds come to his aid; and he has to lie down for about a third of his life to be able to stand or sit the other two thirds.

There he is in bed. The several planes of his inner system which, while he stood, had settled down into an order or scale from the highest to the lowest, are now churned together again. They all lie at the same level. Intuition, thought, emotion, sex—all are now one that earlier, decanted[1] by the vertical position, had been separated for hours.

What have we got to say now, we who had frowned so hard at the Lord for having allowed sex, the instrument of love, to remain so low on the scale of the spine, so close to the excretory regions? It is now His turn to frown at us, unless He smiles with an indulgent humour. There you have him, your man, in bed, again in a level position—in the position of the cow, that which he prefers for love; and he now finds out that in love his faculties, so carefully decanted a while ago, will have to be stirred and mixed together. And how could he reach the fullness of his love were he not to pour all his being into it, from his brain to his sex?

[1] I shall use *decant* to mean the natural grading of liquids by density out of a mixture.

We now realize how shrewd the Creator was Who set the two protagonists of love, brain and sex, at the two ends of the spine so that the whole being had to enter into the game.

And face to face too. For that man and that woman who lie together in a horizontal posture to serve love must, *because they have lived vertically*, meet face-to-face and not, as when they stood on all fours, both facing the earth. In the mating of bull and cow the male sexual parts face the earth and the bull possesses the cow in an anonymous and collective way, as one of the many waves of the sea of the herd; he, in fact, possesses the herd. In the mating of man and woman, the male possesses one particular, definite woman; his sexual parts do not point at the earth but at his mate's; and the two persons are bodily face to face, brain, chest, abdomen; so that when the two partners lie together all their levels blended together, they can reach a fullness of life that nothing else can equal.

Sleep also requires a horizontal position. For in sleep we seek a rest not merely for our bones and muscles, cowish in themselves, bound to live a tree–life during the day, but also for our brain and self, bound to live during our waking hours above and therefore apart from the rest of our being. In our sleep, therefore, we instinctively seek a return to the animal position, our natural and primitive one, in which all our life levels find themselves reunited.

Dreams would then be the outcome of these features of sleep converging as they do into a kind of natural harmony: physical rest, and therefore the release of energies freely to wander in a world wider than that of the senses; the switching off of the lights of the present and the lifting of the curtains that screen from our mental eyes the view of the past and of the future; and the letting ourselves go beyond mere consciousness, whereby the discipline of man erect is relaxed and the hierarchy of his faculties weakened, and in the end abolished, by the dissolution of the up-and-down grading as he passes from the tree to the cow posture.

34

Man cannot do without sleep. This need is more imperious than the mere resting of his muscles would suggest. What man seeks in sleep is not merely bodily rest, i.e. the elimination of the ashes of his motion–machine, but mental rest, i.e. the switching off of his consciousness. It is therefore remarkable that man sleeps at his best when he lies down; for then the decanting of his faculties, which he had achieved by standing up, ceases for the time being; and his intellect, which had set itself above and aloof, is re-absorbed into the whole.

This elevation and separation of the brain is one of the chief consequences of man's assumption of a vertical position. Every triumph of the new creature in his gradual conquest of the universe comes from it; but also a number of shortcomings, frustrations and hardships. The mind of man becomes divorced from life, even from his own life. This split is nowadays recognized and expressed in such modern concepts as the 'conscious' and the 'unconscious'.

Thought, attention, concentration demand an effort from man. This effort measures the violence the human being has to inflict upon himself in order to keep thought apart from life, so that life can be looked at by thought. Thought is an unnatural process. It is as unnatural as standing on two instead of on four feet; and just as some of our bones and muscles hurt still because we insist on standing, so our whole being hurts because we insist on thinking; and just as we had to lie down in order to grant some rest to a body that we have forced to stand against its nature, so we have to go to sleep in order to grant some rest to a soul that we force to split into thought and life.

It is the getting rid of our consciousness that enables us to rest. To rest from what? From our own consciousness. The concertina of our faculties, stretched out by our standing position, is closed again in our sleep. It is this fact which makes sleep such an imperious necessity even when there is no topical reason to cause anxiety to the non-sleeper.

True, the actual content of the mind in certain times of crisis, danger, or distress, may add to the need; but the need for sleep is imperious enough even in normal, even in happy times. Man *must* get rid of his consciousness. He *must* be immersed in his whole self, return to nature, go back to the cow.

It is the sleeper's frequent experience that, as he returns to the shore of wakefulness, he finds it hard at first to orientate his body. He comes from a space devoid of poles and meridians, a space in which all directions are identical, any one as good as any other. Now this is precisely the case also with animal space, even when the animal is awake. For the cow, any direction is as good as any other—a consequence of its horizontal position. On standing erect, however, the biped feels the vertical position to be unique. For a vertical line offers but two directions: up and down. This, in its turn, is of capital importance, for it suggests a scale of values (higher and lower) and an infinitude, neither of which 'stood' out clearly in the horizontal, or animal world.

That something happens to be placed to the left or to the right of another thing lacks significance. (Hence, by the way, the hopeless puerility of valuing political opinions on the basis of right and left, while high and low would have substance even in politics.) But that something be higher or lower does make sense to us. A horizontal distance means nothing in human terms. A vertical distance, much. The All–Farthest means nothing. The All–Highest is our *uppermost* value.

A Creator understood as the All–Highest is hardly a concept that could have been imagined by any but an erect being, a man or a tree, save that the tree has no brains and so no concepts. But the cow, a prisoner of her horizontal position, could not possibly have reached such a concept. It is even doubtful whether the idea of the All–Highest could have

36

been attained by man unaided by his created Creator, before He emancipated Himself and made of His creator His creature. Are we wheeling around wholly within the ambit of man's spirit, or does our circle go beyond it, and are we then, during our outer orbit, letting in a breath of genuine divine freedom? Is that 'Highest' a mere image of the rearing cow at last erect, a prolongation *ad infinitum* of the village totem pole, or some revelation from 'above', emanating from the free spaces of the Deity?

The mere fact that we ask ourselves these questions shows how far man's imagination has travelled upwards since he became erect. *Tu ne me chercherais pas si tu ne m'avais pas déjà trouvé.* But in this search for the Deity, man stretches his spirit towards the zenith for all he is worth and, like the tree ever growing vertical towards the sun, he is led to grow his spiritual stem in as straight a vertical as he can. This vertical yearning of the human spirit may in the end turn out to be the very essence of mankind.

Is it not its very cause? After all, some force there must have been which drove the future man to rise above the easier, lazier, habitual all-fours in order to adopt this inconvenient precarious, easily unbalanced, erect position that even now, thousands of centuries later, makes our bones ache and forces us to lie down for a rest at least every night. What urge, yearning, inspiration impelled him to rise? Whence come? By what or whom powered? The revolution and its consequences reached so incomparably beyond the mere change in stance and in the orientation of the spine, that one is tempted to attribute it to a far higher initiative than any likely to occur to cow, tree, or man.

It is both aspiring and unique. There is an impressive quietness in animals. There they are, set foursquare within their species, content unseeking, unconcerned; each living according to its nature as it found it at birth, and asking no questions. All this conforms with the horizontal posture.

The animal is at rest, in a state of permanent equilibrium. Not so man. His erect posture sets going in him an urge upwards that is doomed to remain forever unassuaged. Ambition, perfection, heroism, holiness, knowledge, mastery, rebellion—this urge upwards will take on many a colour, name, shape, or trend; it will always act as a force stretching the self to its utmost and seeking the All–Highest.

A yearning that exists because its direction is unique. The animal knows no such urge because on the horizontal plane in which he lives there is no privileged, no unique direction. All moves are of equal import. All are nondescript. All are bound to lead to meeting with other members of the herd, or with other herds. All tend to collectivize the individual animal, to drive him out of himself, to pour him out into the lake of the species into which all its individuals are pooled. But on becoming erect man discovers a privileged, unique direction that leads him to no one else but himself and God. Standing on four feet, the quadruped seeks that multitudinous animal, the herd, standing on hundreds of feet, hundreds of willing backs billowing together out of the same sea. While man erect, standing on his narrow base, his two feet close together, stands alone.

From now on, he conquers time. For the herd, the species, consumes its individuals to keep going for centuries until the species also dies. While man erect, escapes through his vertical yearning from the horizontal chain of time, and in seeking the All–Highest, he flies towards eternity.

It seems as if the Creator had been in a hurry to build vertically. Himself born of a vertical philosophy—the All-Highest—He may have felt more akin to erect than to level creations. Thus His first Kingdom, the vegetal, is predominantly vertical. In other words, He thought of the tree before He conceived the cow.

The more intriguing then that when He bethought Himself of the idea of improving on the tree by granting it the boon of mobility, instead of remaining faithful to His up-

38

and-down design, which would have led Him straight to man, He should have taken the retrograde step of launching a horizontal era that doomed Him to the long plodding of the quadrupeds.

It looks as if in His infinite wisdom He had come to the conclusion that, before making a vertical man out of a vertical tree, that all-important creature (who, among his other achievements, was to create Him) should first undergo a long apprenticeship at the school of horizontal life. And who would dare say He was wrong?

Or was it that He had doubts as to whether a gift so risky and adventurous as movement could be so light-heartedly granted? Would a mobile tree be able to keep its balance? After all, the balance of a biped, seen from a time before it actually existed, must have seemed to its Creator as precarious as that of the bicycle to its inventor. Children learn it pretty slowly; old men forget it easily or lose confidence in their command of it, and seek the help of a stick; while friends of the bottle keep dodging it as they can; and as soon as something outward happens to a man, an emotion, an injury, a push, or a shock, the first thing he is apt to lose is his stance; not to speak of women for whom to lose their vertical position is the first and also the last of their resources.

Conjectures. What else can we do? When we attempted to outline that synthesis of cow and tree which man is, the sentence that came to our pen was: 'the spirit of the tree in the body of the cow'. Odd, isn't it? It seems that the wording might, indeed should, have been the very reverse: the spirit of the cow in the body of the tree. The hierarchy natural to us, even if only imbibed at school, would place the animal above the vegetal kingdom. If the spirit is *above* the body . . . well, baffling, isn't it? And yet the fact is obvious: the spiritual pattern of the tree resembles that of the human being, but its corporal design does not—and the very reverse is the case for the cow. Everything that repels us in man seems to us to come from the cow, while we find nothing repulsive about the tree—not even in its organs of procreation, which are so beautiful. The vegetal kingdom does here and there suggest cruel aspects, yet no more than mere forebodings of what in the animal kingdom is going to degenerate into an orgy of ruthlessness. Who doubts but that in creating the animal kingdom the Creator dared a real descent into Hell?

Hell? We had better ask ourselves whether the word fits a world as horizontal as the animal kingdom. The Evil One is so haughty, arrogant, vertical . . ., so much a man! No. The world of animals is not hellish; it does not even attain the infernal and diabolic, for the Devil, after all, *stands up*, and not without a certain greatness inherited from his ancestor Prometheus. Poets have not failed to notice it. Milton, Shelley, Goethe, can hardly conceal their sympathy towards the Devil. And if one but dared . . . that story of Job . . . frankly, doesn't Jehovah betray a certain foible for Satan?

None of this (so-to-speak) anti-God nobility in the sanguinary orgies of sea and forest. And please note that they cannot be dismissed as mere episodes. They are the very principle and basis of animal life, which are no other than terror and death. Every day, at every hour, carnivorous animals sally forth to devour their prey, on whose death they live. And so we are faced with a dilemma: either there is no Creator or the Creator has created this abominable world.

Let us leave atheists for a later page and remain for the present on the second alternative: there is a Creator and He is responsible. It might be argued that our disgust at this scramble of deaths and lives, this life feeding on death, lacks real significance. For instance, there are persons who for no reward on earth would touch or hold a cockroach or eat snails, while many study cockroaches in their laboratories or delight in snails served with garlic and parsley in their best restaurant. That a number of sideshows in the

Lord's world strike us as unpleasant or filthy would then be about as relative and unimportant. There still would remain one disturbing fact: a difference in taste between the Creator and us; and we know full well that nothing works harder against mutual intercourse than differences in standards of taste—let alone an even more disquieting fact, namely that in so asserting our dissent on matters of taste we assume the role of judges over and above the Lord. This in itself would flatter our satanic pride, but it shatters our logic as well as our vanity as creators of the Creator. For we *did* create Him, even though He later emancipated Himself.

A thrush flew from the tree, fluttered for a while over the horns of the cow as if wondering whether they would do for branches to alight on and look around, seemed to reach a negative conclusion and swooped like an eagle on a worm which, with no thought of troubling anybody and with the utmost humility, went crawling along in the grass. A flicker of time, and the thrush was flying upwards victorious, with the unfortunate worm hanging from its beak.

The fact is, though, that these birds . . . they are also bipeds. Their spine is nearly horizontal in some cases, but in most only sloping; as for their neck, it stands up straight, like man's. It seems as if they should have achieved a revolution as spectacular as man's own, and much earlier. Heads high, eyes free . . . but in point of freedom, not merely their eyes. Where could one find more freedom than in these privileged creatures—where a wider horizon, more familiarity with the skies, more scope for movement, more space for initiative?

And yet the winged crowd has given forth nothing in particular. The speeches of the parrot, the laments of the cockatoo, mere curiosities. The order of their collective flights is a mere herd pattern reprinted by and for every generation. Their perfect designs, as lovely when their wings are closed as when they fan out, their colours, feathers, mere herd patterns. The haughty flights of eagle and condor cross the skies without leaving behind the slightest furrow of memory or significance. Ah, yes, but *birds sing*.

In God's creation, only men and birds sing. And this concrete gift, which links them together, does suggest a correlation with the other oddity they share in common: they are bipeds. Is there any logical link between the two oddities? Possibly. As bipeds, men and birds have to struggle with one and the same problem: that of keeping their balance when standing. One of the basic principles of the Lord's world is that three points are necessary to define a plane. In His infinite wisdom the Lord was not content with three feet as a basis for His mobile creatures. There are even some insects to which He granted one hundred—at least in popular entomology; but His minimum and most general figure was four. We all know how unsteady a three-legged table can be, and even a four-legged one if it will fall into lame ways—in other words, if it will waver between the four planes it can choose to stand on by leaving out each time one of its four feet, it can become a nightmare to any office worker or waiter. But if four and three feet prove unstable, what are we to expect of two? So that it is most likely that when the Creator came to the chapter on birds, precursors of man, He would think of endowing them with a sensitive instrument enabling them to keep their balance. This instrument, indispensable for bipeds, is the ear. For both men and birds, therefore, the ear works as the regulator of their stance and balance on the precarious basis of two feet. It is thus seen as natural and by no means odd that birds and human beings should be the two only classes of creatures that sing, i.e. that *have an ear*.

The ear is perhaps the most mathematical of all biological machines. The laws of optics show what an admirable degree of geometrical perfection the human eye has reached; but the ear may well be more perfect still, for it is able accurately to place in outer space the sound it perceives in its own inner space. In order to achieve this natural miracle, the ear registers the three coordinates of the spot where the sound vibrated, by means of the three planes into which the inner ear is shaped; and in order to achieve this astounding result the brain instantaneously resolves three differential equations. The laws of music, such as Ernest Ansermet has defined them in a remarkable book,[1] further illustrate the mathematical substratum of the human ear. Musical perception is based on logarithmic laws, the basis for which is established by auditive consciousness. This is the way Ansermet puts it:

> The system of logarithms from which all musical intervals flow can have no other basis but the harmonic series, the first of which is the octave, but every tonal position can be the origin of one such series and of one such system of logarithms. Every series opens a tonal perspective for the system of logarithms based on it. Our auditive horizon in musical experience must therefore be composed of a fan of similar tonal perspectives between which there will emerge modulating relationships which will allow our auditive consciousness to master the relativity of phenomenal data and to take in at one glance the whole tonal horizon as an organized whole.

It may therefore be permitted to surmise that the bird, since it sings, is already able to sense these recondite mathematical relations, without which its song would lack all meaning; for the height of a note is no mere objective phenomenon; it is a sensation *of* the being, though it acquires a universal value because it obeys identical laws in all men.

We may be touching here on a notable difference between man and bird. Man makes up melodies freely. Every species of bird produces its own specific melody. Its ear would

[1] *Les fondements de la musique dans la conscience humaine.* Neufchâtel, 1963.

43

appear to be capable of sensing one single logarithmic series, and even that reduced to but a few intervals. One is tempted to think that in the divine imagination the bird may have been a mere sketch of what man would later be; perhaps not a very successful one, the Artist having been led astray towards wide, premature ambitions by a powerful flight of His creative urge.[1]

A flight, indeed. What a fascinating temptation the vast spaces of the air must have been for Him. Every creator must have envied Him for being able to bestow on a set of His creatures the freedom of such a three dimensional immensity, to be able to invent natural aviation. No *zeppelins* which, like fishes, go up and down by inflating or deflating a bladder; but from the first day and with no hesitation, a heavier-than-air craft. Of course, we shall need a pair of wings. But where am I to evolve them from? The forward limbs, perhaps. A biped, then? 'What else can I do?', the Lord asked Himself for an answer. And a biped it was. 'Still, he might fall unless I do something about it.

[1] Nevertheless, the musical ability of some birds may be more developed. Here is a report from *The Times* (February 26, 1966):

Someone once called the blackbird the Beethoven of birds, and it certainly does seem to be deliberately composing at times. A phrase is rehearsed and embellished, a line is turned around and tried again, the final vibrato may be sustained a little longer as though the bird were enjoying it all. Dusk, though, is the blackbird's best hour for really mellow song.

I once drew a composer friend's attention to the richness and varied phrasing of blackbird song, and he agreed it had possibilities. It lends itself to transposition to the piano, and we had a fascinating half hour doing just this with our ears cocked on the garden blackbird singing from the television aerial, its favourite song post. This same bird has been with us for years, instantly recognizable by its individual tune with touches of drollery among the calm, mellow notes. It so happens that this bird often hears my wife's cello played through the open French windows on the milder spring days and it seems to have picked up a nice touch or two. Miss Len Howard tells how one of her blackbirds at Ditchling in the South Downs sang a Bach phrase which she felt sure it had learnt from hearing her play the violin.

This report suggests an ability to sing given music by ear, and even a certain ability to compose. It would appear, therefore, to confirm my view on the prophetically human function of the ear of birds.

I'd better see to his ear', His thoughts went on. 'And, of course, he will be a singer'.

All was well now. Was it? His feet and legs, reduced to two, had to be reinforced, and for more than one motive: they would have to bear the weight of the former four; and, in order to spring forward from the ground or from a tree, they would have to develop a good deal of extra energy, let alone that needed to resist the wind while holding on to a branch. Nor is this disquisition on the strength of the bird's legs a mere idle exercise, as will be shown at a later stage.

I was saying that the Creator was unable to resist the temptation to invent natural aviation, an invention that afforded Him so much pleasure that He did not at first tumble to the fact that in evolving the wings out of the forward limbs he actually mutilated the bird. While not in flight the bird is a maimed, armless creature. As soon as He saw him standing on the grass, He realized it and felt aggrieved and set about to correct His error, so far as possible, by endowing birds with strong, clever, selecting and prehensile beaks.

A mere palliative, though. For lack of arms, the bird fell back to the condition of slave of the earth from which his wings seemed to have emancipated him; and so birds give the impression of a permanent contradiction between their wings and eyes, made for infinite space, and their beaks, bent on the earth and its worms. In the eyes of birds there shines already something of that light, sharpened by personality, which foreshadows the eyes of men; while the horny beak goes back to the cow.

One wonders whether the Creator did not conceive the anthropoid simians as a compensation for the failure birds had proved for Him. 'At bottom', He may have thought, 'what birds lack is a good pair of useful and capable forelimbs'. This may well have been the thought with which He

45

started on the creation of the simian family, precisely because when one lands on a new idea one is apt to get enthusiastic about it and to drive it beyond its inherent worth. Had the Lord conceived the idea of an agile arm and an intelligent hand in the normal course of His protean activity, free from any prepossessions, it is most likely that He would have gone on direct from bird to man. But if, as seems to have been the case, He only thought of arm and hand as a corrective for His unfortunate aircraft experiment and so to speak to atone for having mutilated the bird, He must have over-reached Himself and that is how He created four-handed beings.

What is the good of the hind-hands which quadrumana display? Little if any, as the popular imagination has not failed to observe and to register in stories. A monkey and a parrot are having an argument on their respective abilities, and the monkey holds forth on his agile movements and gymnastic achievements, whereupon after listening to him for a long while, the parrot superciliously replies: 'What's all that worth? I can speak.' And the monkey retorts: 'But what have I been doing these fifteen minutes?'

This flying off at a tangent reveals that the general concensus sees the activities of the monkey as, at most, good for entertaining children. His hind-hands are no good to him. Not only are they practically useless; they have hindered him in his evolution towards an erect posture which, together with his fore-hands, might have raised him to manhood. And now is the moment to recall how important it is for the biped that the two pillars on which he has to stand be strong enough as a basis and as a catapult as well. Agile and subtle hands are of little avail when no solid basis of feet and legs is provided. The evolution towards man determined in the simian by the birth of the hand fails—owing to an excess of hands. And yet the Lord knew already that two hands are enough to sharpen the wits of a creature, for He had achieved it in the squirrel.

At last, through the usual processes of trial and error, the Lord came to creating man. The problem was clear. He had to 'tree' the quadruped without any more beating about the bush with monkeys and birds. This meant strengthening his hind-legs and, in particular, the pedestal type of function in his feet; freeing his hands so as to make them fit to be the instruments of a brain raised to the apex of the organism, and empowering him to see outwards and inwards.

Thus begins the wonderful play of the three prehensile organs: hand, eye, and brain, the instruments of intellectual captation, below the spiritual captation, intuition, and above the corporal captation, instinct. The work of mutual education going on through the life of the individual and of the species between hand, eye and brain is a common-place in the history of men. But precisely because of its success, perhaps unequalled in creation, it raises a question already met with in this disquisition: Who—what drove the quadruped to rear or tree himself, not merely to make a scene and return to his normal foursquare, but for good and forever to stand erect?

It is not likely to have been because one day the cow or the horse bethought itself of freeing his forward feet from the slavery of the earth. In the long trek of the four-footed ones across the ages, when and why did one of them make up his mind to stand up on its rear legs and keep standing in such an uncomfortable, unsteady and unnatural position? How did this branch of evolution begin, incomparably the most radical of all and the most pregnant with future unpredictable developments? Does that slogan about the survival of the fittest apply to this case? Shall we recall how ridiculous it seemed to us as an explanation for the kaleido-scopic fan of the peacock or for the supercilious speeches of the parrot?

Not even as a rationalist can we respect anyone who will deny that at this precise moment in the evolution of life some transcendental events took place, beyond mere mathematics, physics, or chemistry; an act of intention, imagination, creativeness; an initiative which foresaw that the human ear would have to be able instantly to integrate three differential equations, and that the emancipated hand would raise the intellectual function of the brain to unsuspected heights.

For what then happened was that, owing to the decanting effect of the vertical posture, the brain was severed from vegetative and emotional life to such an extent that it began to conceive something totally new: *comprehension*, that is, the recreation of Creation into a pure scheme or system wholly free from any emotion or animal influence. The time will come to elucidate whether this attempt is valid, and whether man gains or loses by entering into it. For the moment let us be content with emphasizing the newness and the nobility of the attempt as such.

It will lead to yet another of those patterns of order the designing of which we saw as the favourite and typical occupation of man erect. This time, man is not seeking to create the Creator; he aims at recreating Creation, projecting into it his own intellect as a photographic image. The invention of a pattern, certainly; yet not as heretofore free but subject to an exacting law. The pattern he is trying to imagine must exactly fit the outer world as he sees it and as it works. We are after Knowledge. This is a move, an urge that presupposes the rise of the head above the level of the rest, the standing up of the whole figure, the 'treeing' of the quadruped.

Who wished this evolution or revolution? Did the Creator actually wish to give himself a judge and even an inquisitor? Was it He who secretly infused into the four-footed animal the desire to tree itself? And if not, how are we to explain that a four-footed animal should ever have been moved to achieve such an unnatural and even ridiculous performance?

We have already shown that on the basis of modern

physics it is possible to prove that there is no such a thing as matter, and that the whatever-it-is which under that name bruises our forehead or our shinbones is pure intelligent energy. Or at least energy obedient to intellectual laws. If the spirit, therefore—in other words, intelligent energy—is the very substance of the universe, then only the spirit can be the moving agent of evolution. It follows that it was the spirit which urged the quadruped to rise on two feet since thanks to this revolution animal evolution rises to the level of the highest form of the spirit by incarnating in the two-handed biped—its most active, its *only* active instrument under the creator.

Somewhat dogmatic, though, that conclusion. How do we know that in this universe soaked in mystery man is the only active instrument of the spirit? And I am not thinking of intelligent beings that may exist on other planets of our own or some other solar system. I am thinking rather of beings that may exist higher up in the hierarchy between man and God. That Sunday-school pyramid rising from stones to plants, animals, men, and God strikes one as a bit too simple, too anthropomorphic and tainted with human vanity. It seems more reasonable to think that, since the distance between men and God is so unimaginable, this immense space can hardly be empty and must surely be peopled by intermediate categories of living beings. The trouble is that positively and immediately we see and know no other categories than our own and those below, while the Creator is only known to us through His works—and, worse still, those of His works that we know do not always enhance His prestige in our eyes.

Now this is where our intermediate categories come in. Haven't we grumbled against the Creator? The ugliness in His world; the cruelty in His world; that mistake of giving wings to the birds at the expense of their arms; the four hands of the monkey . . . But suppose the Creator we are discussing and finding fault with were not actually the Supreme Spirit in person but some sort of 'subcreator' or 'lieutenant creator' of those we suspect may be lurking in that vast space which separates us from God? Or, in other words, when man, indulging in his favourite pastime, that of designing patterns, thought he had created the Creator, all he had done was to find a Being, no doubt still powerful enough, yet not quite what newspapermen now like to call 'the summit'?

This was, if I remember right, a favourite idea with Anatole France, who though he died saying that he believed in nothing, did find some fascination in playing with faith. It is a reasonable idea. The universe is so big . . . The Spanish Empire was a good deal smaller, yet Philip II would not have been able to govern it without viceroys. True, the All–Highest, save for a number of historians (who happen to be devout Catholics), is an incomparably bigger person than Philip II; but the universe is just as infinite as He. Then why not imagine that God delegates to the care of 'Vicegods' the creation of certain zones of the universe that He does not want or is not able to attend to?

Not a few problems would thus be solved, and not a few mysteries cleared as well. Our disapproval of the Lord's world would turn out to be a disapproval of the world botched by the particular vicegod in charge of our affairs; and faced with vice-divine misdemeanours, we should always be able to appeal to the Lord as the Indian subjects of Queen Victoria appealed to her against the rule of her viceroy. Those awkward errors we observed with regard to birds and monkeys, that joke about the parrot, all those near-human weaknesses and contingencies which had seemed as if they might impair the divine majesty would after all not rise above the vice-divine court. A hope would remain.

More than one hope. For it is obvious that man shall never reach the infinitely high level of God; yet the hope is not forbidden to him of aspiring to become the vicegod of some passable Barataria Island that the Lord might have available in the Milky Way, in a galaxy not too far out into the open. We cannot get reconciled to the idea that between God and ourselves there is nothing better than a desert devoid of all creatures. The Holy Roman Catholic Church has wisely peopled this space with saints, angels, and archangels. We would only wish to add to this picture an amendment possibly inspired by Sancho Panza. We had rather that the superhuman beings who people the space that separates us from the Creator did not limit themselves to hanging about parasitically, like courtiers 'round the throne of the Lord; but that they took their share of the responsibilities of the government of the universe. Something of this kind must have inspired those services and institutions which have chosen saints as patrons. It does not seem, however, that in this case, at any rate, democratic elections from below have always led to fortunate results. It would be rash, for instance, to surmise how the archangel Gabriel received his designation as patron of television. It looks, therefore, as if it might be best to await valid appointments coming from on high. We should not mind being always ruled by governors designated by the Divine Court, since they would be more carefully chosen. Sooner or later, just as the Creoles of Peru or New Spain, we should proclaim our independence. But, of course, after a very long time. And even then we might be told that we were past praying for.

# 3

The tree and the cow, the vertical and the horizontal, remain the two coordinates of man's life. They command the primary impulses behind his doing, thinking, feeling. Sometimes they act together; at other times one or the other will predominate and man's happenings will take on a style ruled by either 'vertical' or 'horizontal' impulses.

That vertical urge which is man, no matter how or by whom initiated, is after all incarnated in an animal and belongs, therefore, to a species that, as such, is under the sway of a horizontal impulse on which it depends for its life and, therefore, for that of its individuals. Were man nothing more than a vertical urge, he would have died out, a mere oddity in Creation. For the species to remain and endure, animal, collective, horizontal tendencies are indispensable in order to counterbalance that unique urge skyward. Man lives thus in a continuous dynamic equilibrium between his vertical and his horizontal worlds, between solitude and multitude.

And here we come across one of those paradoxes of which nature seems to be so fond. Yes, the vertical posture has separated the several vital levels, but the vertical impulse that caused it tends to keep them united, threaded together (so to speak); while there lives in man, even when already decanted into several levels, a definite horizontal tendency (possibly a hang-over from his four-footed life) that incites him to live flat along every one of his 'storeys', or in other words, to accept the decantation and separation of his several levels with a cowish placidity.

We shall therefore have to discriminate between *what* is

lived and *how* it is lived. On any level observed, some will live it horizontally and others vertically; and it is a fact, though perhaps paradoxical and odd at first, that life will be more fully human if and when the individual succeeds in preserving at each level the taste and touch of the other ones.

The intellectual, for instance, is a man who preferably lives at the level of his conscious mind. But much depends on whether he lives this level under the sway of a horizontal or of a vertical tendency. The first will lead to a dry, deductive, rationalistic type of intellectual, a skilful manipulator of the arguing machine, who will explain everything but understand nothing. The second will be able to fecundate his intellect with his intuition and, owing to his unimpaired link with his affective and sensitive planes, he will keep open a perspective towards a fuller horizon for his life.

A similar observation applies to the affective life of man. The vertical posture separates love from thought on the one hand, and from the animal instincts on the other. So we see horizontal intellectuals who reveal themselves as beings unfit for love (even for intellectual love); and persons endowed with a rich affectivity who seem unable either to express it through ideas or to pour it out in passions; and bodies whose sense of what they call love is such that they do not rise above animal mating. Only those who have not merely adopted the vertical position but also maintained in their beings its original upward impetus are capable of enjoying human love in all its gamut from the level of instinct to that of intuition.

How neatly could this picture be rounded off by showing that moral–social urges come from the horizontal, animal stage of man, while religious yearnings spring from his human, erect position. But the facts will not oblige. Whence that irresistible tendency of men afflicted with religion to lie on their fronts in the fullest horizontal position they can command? How can we dismiss the stiff-necked, unyielding, erect stand of the puritan moralist?

We had better, therefore, reconcile ourselves to the view that in both morality and religion we are to meet a blend of animal–horizontal–herd and human–vertical–personal tendencies. The term 'mores' itself is so vague, so apt to carry different meanings, that it makes the issue as easy to discuss as it makes it hard to understand. By its root, it suggests custom, 'what one does', i.e. what *everybody* does, therefore herd behaviour. This thumb-rule of practical conduct looks no higher than the eyes of the species, at most, the level of its billowing spines. It is called empiricism by those who try—successfully?—to endow it with respectability. (The notion that the word 'empiricism' comes from 'empire' is, unfortunately, rejected by all professional etymologists.) Empiricism is evidently a horizontal or animal form of morality, and though it can be as stiff-necked as a bulldog, it is not erect—not, at any rate, more erect than a horse rearing. In other words, empiricism is four-footed, and those who call it pedestrian are indulging in understatement, a form of inexactitude-by-common-consent that is only permitted to Englishmen.

Empiricism is not erect because if it were it would glance far afield in the manner of shepherds, while short or at most middle distances are the favourite scope of the empiricist, in the manner of a cow, or even of a bull, no matter his Christian name. The empiricist instinctively knows that in the long run the herd is safe, for nature sees to that. He need only attend to the average behaviour of 'everybody' at the present time. His instinct precludes him from raising his eyes higher than the level of the herd. The empiricist is the perfect nationalist.

That is why nations tend to conceive themselves as animals, this one as a lion, that one as a tiger, the one beyond as a leopard, an eagle, a bear, and even a kangaroo. It is only too obvious that those collective human beings we call nations linger still in the cannibal phase of their evolution, since they are still apt to devour each other not only shamelessly but with an unbounded admiration for their own digestive powers. Doubts on this score will vanish after a glance at the world maps of 1939 and 1950 showing the number of nations that the Soviet Union and China devoured in the interval. There can be no doubt that nationalism is primarily animal and horizontal.

But as soon as other purely herd tendencies begin to make themselves felt in human behaviour, the influence of the vertical posture will become manifest. Intellectual and aesthetic motivations will appear that endow human actions with a depth and a subtlety that a mere herd-morality could not supply.

The first of these will probably be an assertion of the self. Solitude versus multitude. The herd is all very well, but there is also the self, standing erect in a vertical line rising from the centre of the earth up to the zenith, the abode of the All-Highest. And this line, a man truly erect cannot and will not renounce for any herd on earth. Man's fidelity to his own vertical becomes a rule of morality. A rule? Hasn't that word smuggled itself from the animal-horizontal-herd world of empiricism into our human-vertical-personal world? It cannot be a mere rule that another rule may push aside. Fidelity to one's own vertical is not merely inflexible but essential, consubstantial with the person.

Of course, there may be men—there *are* men—who do not resist the herd-horizontal trend for whom fidelity to the vertical line, though normally strong, may not be so exacting, so consubstantial with their persons as to be capable of resisting the call of the herd. From such men strong nations may be expected to emerge; for in their communities the collective pull is sure to defeat the individual pull when it comes to behaviour. A nation thus composed of men whose horizontal pull can win over their vertical yearning will

55

more thoroughly consume its men. Its citizens, in their turn, will deem themselves fortunate to be consumed by their nation. Morality will tend to be empirical, and the feeling of nationality will be stronger than that of humanity.

This tremendous inversion of values often occurs in nations of Germanic stock, and in recent times gave rise to the monstrous aberration of nazism. Monstrous precisely because it was aberrant. Nazism was a typical case of herd-movement. Nearly a generation after Hitler's death those of his wretched followers who had to answer for their past crimes before the law courts would still seek an excuse in 'the duty to obey'. The 'shepherd' of that herd was a 'vertical' person. Over that there can be no doubt. But what did he see? *Blut und Boden*. Blood and earth. Poor man, he was a tree upside down, his foliage and branches sunk into the earth and his blind roots up in the air. And his All–Highest was the All–Lowest, Satan. Nazism was a satanic religion.

Yet, *a caveat*. For it to propagate so quickly and to strike roots so deeply in the whole people, and so gifted a people at that, a minimum of predisposition must be posited. Without offence, rather with admiration for the noble endeavour of the Federal Republic to uproot the evil, one might formulate the psychological situation of 1933 by saying that Hitler reached the summit because there were too many Germans who were nazi-germ carriers.

This unfortunate situation may be due to the composition of two tendencies, one gregarious or horizontal, the other vertical but upside down. Of all Europeans, the German is the most gregarious or, in our language, the most horizontal. Further on, we may see this conclusion confirmed from another approach. He is moreover the European most heavily incarnated, the one who needs the greatest amount of body to lodge his spirit. Are there any statistics providing the average of total weight of peoples and nations? At any rate, to judge at first glance, one may risk the opinion that

56

the German people are the heaviest in the world, both in stature and in corpulence.

This abundance of flesh in the German does not express itself necessarily in a corresponding exuberance of sexual life. Indeed, it does seem that German sexuality is rather blurred and confused. A people that makes the sun feminine and the moon masculine can hardly be said to hold clear notions about sex. The overpowering incarnation of the German will then seek to flow out in other ways, the chief of which might well be the assertion of the herd, the importance granted to blood and earth, the inversion of the vertical.

Nor should we fall into the exaggeration (which would also be an oversimplification) of presenting the people that gave forth Goethe and Beethoven merely as an inverted vertical tree, its foliage hidden in the earth, its roots naked in space. The German nation may well be proud of having endowed the world with as many lofty intuitions as any other. What sets it apart is a kind of ambivalence in its vertical posture that turns out to be as typical as its sexual ambivalence. The German, therefore, is:

—more gregarious than the other Europeans;

—more vacillating in his verticality between the positive or upward and the negative or downward positions.

These might well be the causes of the racial arrogance of the Germans, which has cost them so many humiliations.

The English character is not altogether free from some of these features. The predominance of the herd over the individual has never perhaps been better put both in words and in deeds than by some Englishmen. A Canadian statesman once revealed that during one of his visits to London, Churchill the Great had advised him thus: 'Never stand if you can sit, never sit if you can lie down.' A clear directive from the leader of a horizontal people for whom the vertical position is not natural. The golden dream of every Englishman is to lie down; if possible, on the grass. You may see

57

them, crowds of them, lying on the grass in their wonderful parks as soon as a pale sun, trembling with cold, pierces the clouds; or by the thousands in parallel lines of long chairs along the fresh, bitter lace of the sea, breathing with delight the salty air blended with the smoke of their mutual pipes; and above all, doing absolutely nothing but ruminate. Cows, happy cows in their (at last) horizontal position and in the bosom of nature. Or had you perhaps fancied that there was nothing but mere caprice in dubbing the Englishman John Bull?[1]

Nevertheless, this horizontal tendency, though so strong in the Englishman that it has enabled him to create the most united herd in history, has not misled him into the diabolical racialism that has tempted the Germans at times. It would seem that when the German sacrifices himself for the herd he is thinking of blood and earth; while the Englishman in such a trance is thinking of something less animal. When Captain Scott dies in the antarctic solitude, 'proud of dying like an Englishman', he offers the world a stoic example of the victory of the herd's horizontal force over the individual vertical. Yet his attitude does suggest a vertical rigidity, as if Scott said: 'I die standing and for God. My God is my country'.

Ultravertical people do not like this attitude. It seems to them that Scott might have said: 'I am proud to die like a man'. After all, beyond the bar of death there are no

[1] The vigour of the horizontal attitude in the Englishman's subconscious can be gathered from the fact that while the rising of a four-footed animal on its hind legs is described in French as *se cabrer* and in Spanish *encabritarse* (i.e. rising to fight like a he-goat) and as *sich bäumen* in German and *enarbolarse* in Spanish (i.e. yearning towards heaven like a tree), it is described in English as *rearing*. Thus the English do not see the head seeking heaven but the rear seeking the earth. This peculiar broaching of the subject from hindquarters is not without significance. This significance is increased if we consider the meaning of the word *ahead*. For a man erect, it should mean aloft. It means forward. The animal horizontal attitude is obvious. That this semantic twist may be due to the perspective of a nation of riders would not appear in any way to weaken the value of the observation.

Englishmen; there are only men. Still, the herd is not enough to explain this stand. Scott was to the very end faithful to his own vertical; but the apex of his vertical was not the All–Highest. It was his country. After all, he was an Anglican.

It would be hard to deny that this attitude is by no means miles away from that of the incipient nazi or pre-nazi whose vertical line has gone upside down and, through earth and blood, points straight at Satan. Rise towards heaven and just stop at the fatherland? Still, for the Englishmen England is no mere thing of blood and earth. Merely to compare his monosyllables with those heavy German trains of letters loaded with syllables and consonants is enough to realize that the Englishman does not feel his country or his people as something carnal and corporeal. Rather should we conceive his image of it as one of the many 'delegations' which the Englishman entrusts to his country.

This had better be explained. Belonging as he does to the most perfect herd the ages have ever witnessed, the Englishman is wont to delegate to the herd a number of aspects of his personality—generally the worst. Selfishness, power-lust and wealth, cunning and other evil arts, he loads on the shoulders of his country. Hence his excellent and well deserved fame as a person. It might well turn out that in stopping short of the summit to be content with his country as the apex of his yearning, the Englishman, so used to 'delegating', takes it for granted that his country will eventually take care of the rest of the ascent, on behalf of him and of all his countrymen, up to the Creator Himself. This would amount to assuming that England is one of those vicedeities to which, in His turn, the Lord delegates the government of a part of the world—an assumption not perhaps quite as absurd as it looks.

There are other European types in whom the vertical

59

component is stronger. Man erect, by dint of fidelity to his own vertical line rising straight towards the All–Highest, realizes the essential value of every other vertical line. The beginnings of another form of herd, a herd vertical? By no means. For here there is no pouring of each into the pool of all, but a mere sense that 'there goes one like me'. There, however, *out* there, not mixed with me.

The limits of the herd are not for such a man. He is far more of an individual than a citizen, national, subject of the nation to which he happens to belong. His morality contains a stronger element of fidelity to his own self than of rules of good citizenship or public service. Not that such rules need be absent from his morality. But they will be there not so much on their own merits as insofar as they happen to be a part of his personal life philosophy. Nor is this a matter of interests—mine against those of the community. Indeed, since 'vertical' behaviour springs from sources independent of the herd, we have been led to suspect in its motivation the influence of the personal ideas and feelings of the individual concerned. The morality of mankind would have remained stuck forever in a herd-like conservatism but for the individual ideas of its more vertical members who dared defy custom.

Furthermore, there is in every erect man an inherent standard of taste. It covers every act of his life; from the way he dresses to the way he thinks, lives, and behaves. Ultimately, it might well be that the morality of erect (not necessarily of upright) men is ruled by taste at least as much as by habit or principle; and even that, of the three, taste may in many cases be the strongest.

*It is done. It should be done. I do not do that.* These are the three roots of our moral behaviour. The first is collective. It stands for morality in the primary sense, meaning 'the ways of the herd'. The second is individual in that it appeals to the court of reason, an instance above the herd, whose authority emanates from the top of man erect—his head.

No. It is not collective, not herd-born. It is universal, because all 'verticals' recognize it. The third is strictly individual. It appeals to taste, a purely personal experience that can neither be shared nor transmitted, and is not easy to put into words. Of the three, therefore, taste is perhaps the most vertical.

But life is so subtle. Habit, principle, and taste have ultimately to rely on the individual will that brings them to bear on the surface of events; and this surface may resist. A challenge may arise; an obstacle may bar the way; a rival force may endeavour to break the habit, infringe the principle, offend the taste. Then, what happens? The individual will is sure to struggle; and the actual feeling in the resister will be one of stiffening, of hardening of the spine, of standing erect, of straightening the vertical.

We thus return to the contrast between the uniqueness of the vertical and the plurality of the horizontal; itself latent beneath the contrast between the flow of tradition and the springs of new life; or between polycracy and monocracy; or between bridge–men and tower–men—themes that recur in one form or another throughout human history.

A nation may be likened to a river of life; and the waves of the water flowing down the slope of time call to mind the movement of a herd at a trot. Tradition, the continuity of the nation, is thus in fact the flow or march of the herd in the riverbed of time—a typically horizontal motion, slightly downwards, as the second law of thermodynamics commands for everything that flows.

But the flow of the life of the nation would soon dry up, if only because of the evaporation of its spirit, were it not enriched every day by the springs of new water supplies on the riverbed of time during the present, the contribution of the creative spirits of its people while they are alive. This is a vertical force.

Thus, in the end, the life of the nation is the outcome of

these two forces: a tradition, carrying down from the past into the future the spirit of past generations in a horizontal drive; and the creative power of the generation actually alive, springing upwards in a powerful surge.

In some nations the traditional drive is stronger than the new creative power. In other words, some nations are more horizontal than vertical. Others are the other way about. And the proportion between the two forces may, of course, change in time. In some cases the springs surging from the riverbed will but with difficulty be able to rise owing to the massive power of tradition rolling overhead. This is the case with gregarious nations, endowed with a strong collective or horizontal sense. A typical example might be Germany. At times this gregarious sense might be fostered by the predominance of a horizontal ideology such as communism; and the present-day creative spirits would be the less able to contribute their springs of life water to the traditional flow of their nation's culture. The tragic case of Pasternak may be recalled among many less well-known, though not less tragic, cases. Whether naturally caused or artificially fostered, the massive, horizontal drive in the gregarious nations will swiftly absorb the creative springs that it receives from the day alive, and curb them into the general traditional flow.

Other nations, on the contrary, possess a relatively poor horizontal drive. Their tradition is weak. Their present-day creative springs rise freely, pierce the thin current of tradition, and fuse into the air to shine in the sun with their individual originality, hardly affected by the common drive, so that they leave but little of their water of life to flow along the river of tradition for future generations. This is, for instance, the case of Spain. These nations are more prone to anarchy than to communism.

Compare the weight of common thought that Hamlet or Faust carry within their weary foreheads with the utter freedom from any collective bond with which Don Quixote or Don Juan move about on the world stage. How deeply we feel that Hamlet and Faust, barely sprung from the river-beds of their respective national traditions, have been curbed, assimilated, made to flow in the herd-like, many-backed movement of the national progress towards some future form of the collective culture very much the same as the present and past; while the two Spaniards, springing with an almost volcanic vigour, shoot through the thin current of tradition and fuse in many-coloured, fanciful shapes in the thin air of the day. Their lives remain un-absorbed, unassimilated by the traditional flow of their country, and so they rise to a level of universal culture less as definite characters with a national background (like Faust or Hamlet) than as symbols of certain moods and forces of all mankind.

The strain is there throughout. Faust and Hamlet struggle desperately to save their vertical yearning from the massive flow of tradition that in the end drowns them; Don Quixote feels the lack of horizontal, herd-like forces around him, and tries to imagine them so powerfully indeed that he turns two flocks of sheep into armies, peoples, nations. Obviously, here Cervantes pokes fun at the nationalism of his contemporaries, which he shrewdly symbolizes as the behaviour of herds. This adds force and point to the dis-coveries of Rodríguez Marín, who has proved that behind the pompous, comic names of the knights Don Quixote sees leading the two flocks into combat there lurk the historical characters who are prominent in the battle of the Armada. As for Don Juan, his vertical pressure is so high that he cannot tolerate the idea of any wall, door, law, obstacle, limitation to his boundless energy. Of all human symbolic figures, Don Juan is perhaps the most uncompromisingly vertical, the most vigorous if not the loftiest tree.

History echoes what literature has uttered. Even if a period is chosen such as the Elizabethan when England is at its most vertical, what strikes the observer when comparing the English and the Spaniards of those days is precisely the predominance of the cow in the former and of the tree in the latter. The Englishman, even Drake, even Raleigh, splendidly vertical as they are, assume a horizontal, herd-like, traditional attitude as their exploits become integrated into the flow of national events. Drake's 'Golden Hynd' becomes the Bank of England—an unthinkable event in the history of Spain and her conquistadors. For these conquistadors were not bridges, like the English, leading from an English past to an English future; they were towers, each a tower of his own, rising high from the ground up, leading nowhere, being but not becoming, seeking the achievement of the pure vertical self.

Extreme cases both, no doubt. But don't you perceive here a far deeper, more substantial explanation of the historical evolution of the two countries than the official ones? Who could have guessed in 1550 that Britain would become the leading nation of the nineteenth century, and Spain sink to third power rank? And what a wealth of causes to account for it all—economic, religious, political . . . But the cause of all these causes, is it not to be found in that the English horizontal, herd, traditional impulse is more powerful than the Spanish, so that the life of England is in the end a river made up of waves that are the lives of myriads of Englishmen who drown themselves in that natural river which is England; while the Spaniards, every one of them, refuse to flow into each other to make the life-river of Spain; for they rise like towers, each a separate vertical, seeking to achieve his own elevation and touch the sky with his own hands—cow versus tree.

But please, do not imagine that this is meant to mean that the tree must be preferred to the cow. Life, subtle as ever, would have a good laugh at us. The finest man must surely be the one whose tree-like tendencies are strengthened and enriched by vigorous memories of his cow-life; in other words, that one who is rich in both vertical and horizontal forces and holds them in harmony. When we have detected vertical and horizontal trends in a man and even hinted at their relative strength, we have said nothing about their absolute value. Beethoven may be—I believe he is—more horizontal than vertical; while Goya is more vertical than horizontal. And yet I suspect that Beethoven is more vertical than Goya simply because, being altogether a bigger man, he can afford to take in more of the cow while remaining a taller tree than the Spaniard.

This applies to many Englishmen, too. They are richly endowed with a social sense that comes straight from the herd. Nothing is more striking than the inner power of the herd that every Briton feels, and which rings vigorously in that most English of words: 'Us'. But he knows little of the English who has not had occasion to admire the full power of the vertical personality in many of them. I have often felt like returning to them in this respect the compliment Wordsworth paid us Spaniards when, in a famous sonnet, having described men of 'patience and temperance, with this high reserve, honour that knows the path and will not swerve' (a wonderfully vertical line!), he adds 'such men of old were England's native growth: and throughout Spain (thanks to high God) forests of such remain'. Note the tree-like vertical mood of the whole poem, not forgetting that '*high* God' Who hovers above the tallest of trees.

So high, indeed, that the phrase seems to settle *a priori* that religion is a purely vertical urge. Shall we assent? Perhaps . . . on condition that we keep 'religion' in the singular. That religion is vertical does not seem to admit of any doubt. But as for *religions* . . . that is quite another theme, and one that lends itself only too well to argument. To begin with, we have already had occasion to meet one, *nazism*, which while not altogether lacking in a vertical element, inverted it, aiming it at the All-Lowest,

Satan; its main trend, however, being horizontal and herd-like.

From the cow, also, comes the other modern mass religion, communism—and this time only from the cow. It would hardly be fair to say as much of Marxism, for Marx was animated by a vigorous liberal (therefore vertical) impulse, manifest if not in his economic, at any rate, in his political views. One might even be tempted to describe him as a liberal heart served (or betrayed) by a socialist head. One may differ from him as to ways and means, as to the strategy and the tactics of the holy war he declares, but hardly as to his liberal aim, which is no other than the liberation of man.

Communism sought to raise Marx to the first place in its trinity of prophets—now reduced to a duality since Stalin was hurled down to Hell by his own high priests. But this invocation of Marx is one of the many impostures of the Soviet heresy. Communism as practised by the Soviet Union, China, and their respective satellites is a horizontal and gregarious religion devoid of the slightest trace of a vertical urge. It aims at the levelling down of everyone to the level of the mass, to the submission of all vertical spirits and of every vertical trend in every spirit to the horizontal line of the herd. It persecutes as an 'enemy of the people' anyone who would dare stray from the path mapped out by the shepherd; and in its vocabulary no word is considered more abominable than 'deviationist'. Could there be a more horizontal term? Deviationist—he who strays from the herd. On the horizontal field of indifferent directions, communism singles out and chalks a certain line that the herd must follow. But this singling out is wholly artificial, and entirely due to the will of the boss who happens to wield the shepherd's staff. When the boss changes, the line changes . . . Meanwhile, woe to him who deviates. And if no one can dare deviate, choosing a different horizontal direction than that chalked out on the grass, what will

66

befall the unhappy one who will dare 'tree' himself in search of a vertical?

Passing now from these social–political para-religions of our day to the classical, traditional forms of true religion, we may expect to observe in them a more or less clear and conscious tension between the horizontal, collective, animal trends and the vertical impetus that directs every individual towards the spirit. We have already guarded against any tendency to identify the former with morality and the latter with religion. The tension will express itself differently in different religions, and even within the same religion in different environments.

If, for instance, we compare the two great Asian religions, we may suspect that they differ mostly in two of their aspects: Buddhism is more clearly and explicitly a monotheistic religion than Vedantism or Hinduism—to such an extent, indeed, that by dint of stripping the deity of physical attributes it has called forth unmerited suspicions of atheism. Vedantism, on the other hand, even though possibly grounded on a monotheistic philosophy, tolerates such a proliferation of gods as to amount in practice to polytheism.

This contrast may be deeper than it seems. To begin with, Buddhism stands on a purer vertical or spiritual position than Vedantism; it does not scatter its upward impetus towards various gods. With the Hindus, monotheism is an attitude left to the brahmin or shepherd, not for the benefit of their sheep. The ordinary herd follows the several gods within a horizontal religion, like cows or sheep trotting towards their drinking troughs, while the brahmins alone seek the pure spirit above or beyond the veil of appearances. Furthermore, the respective attitudes of Buddhism and Vedantism towards the outer world, though at first sight not unlike, are in fact different. Buddhism seeks to liberate the single being from any bond that ties him with the world and the flesh by making him concentrate on God and longing for union with Him; while Vedantism does not deny the world, rather does it affirm it and brings out the importance of Karma, the chain of cause and effect that binds man to life, and not only to this one but to a number of more lives to come, as successive forms in an age-long spiritual schooling. This idea, transmigration, could not be more horizontal, since it carries on the trotting of the herd for centuries of centuries. Vedantism would then appear to be predestined to turn the cow into a sacred animal.

Though Buddhism seems to have absorbed from Vedantism a certain amount of belief in transmigration, the contrast between the two faiths is fairly clear. Buddhism, in its urge for purification, seems to endeavour to escape towards the zenith of the spirit, negating or rejecting all lower levels—intellectual, affective, animal. Vedantism, on the other hand, remains integrally human and, though it prescribes control and discipline over the lower levels, it wishes them to be granted their share of life.

In practice, especially among the crowd, both religions are apt to be afflicted by the superstitious degeneracy that few confessions are able to avoid—a sure sign, if not in the faith at any rate in the faithful, of a weak vertical impetus and a predominance of horizontal forces. This might also be the cause of the caste system as well as a certain tendency to the worship of sex notable in Vedantism. In Buddhism the deformation would rather take the form of clericalism (if that be the word to refer to brahmin predominance), a defect not to be observed in Vedantism.

We might dwell a bit on this phenomenon, clericalism, if only because it is in fact one of the many forms under which the tension between the horizontal and the vertical forces may be observed. In religion, the essential fact is the yearning towards a transcendent God on high, emanating from the immanent God within. It is a purely individual tendency, which becomes universal because God is one and only one for all men; therefore, a tendency universal only in God. In us, and while it subsists as a mere yearning, it remains purely individual.

This is the field of individual yearnings over which the prophet–founder of a religion operates. A given group of yearnings, set in a concrete system of circumstances defined in time and space, will eventually allow itself to be polarized so as to take on a certain form, colour, style. A 'faith' is born, no longer the mere pure religious yearning that was there before, but this yearning decorated and overloaded with a number of ideas, affections, and traditions given forth in part by the prophet–founder, in part by the mass or people that follow him. The prophet, a vertical shepherd, casts his influence over the people, a horizontal cattle; and thus a confession or 'religion' is born in whose bosom the usual tensions will be set going between the horizontal and the vertical forces in man. The prophet–shepherd will generate a body of shepherds, guardians of the ideas, affections, and traditions of the faith, and these shepherds will collegiate into a church. The church will soon find that it needs a sacristy. Here are then the three aspects of the religious tragedy that reappears in ever changing forms, in ever the same substance throughout the ages and nations: faith creates the church, the church creates the sacristy, the sacristy serves the church, the church serves the faith. That is meant to be so. But action equals reaction; and so, in time, it will turn out that the faith will serve the church, and the church will serve the sacristy. What had been born as a vertical yearning scatters in horizontal errands.

This scheme of things fits the three western religions. Judaism may well be the most intensely bent on the search for pure spirit. Not in vain are the Jews prominent among the finders or discoverers of monotheism, and not in vain is their religion the stem from which branch out both Christianity and Islam. The austerity of their worship, their disdain for merely outward and adventitious elements, their concentration on a personal link with God, their very pudicity about the use of the name of the deity, are vertical features. They, nevertheless, live in a permanent tension with horizontal, gregarious trends, such as their zealous fidelity to the law and the prophets, and the tough, millennial customs and traditions to which this people owe their survival.

The wonderful blossoming of mystic poetry that Islam has given forth should bar any overhasty denial of the existence of a vigorous vertical spirit among Muslims. It would appear, nevertheless, not unfair to consider the Quran as the least spiritual of the sacred books of the religions of the West. Islam gives free rein to the carnal and sensuous elements in man, and its notion of holy war does rest for a good part on assumptions of an obviously herd-like and horizontal nature.

As for Christianity, as it shines in the Gospels, it was obviously born on a purely vertical impulse. Christ may well be the most purely vertical spirit in history. His whole yearning tends towards the All-Highest. He dies on his feet, and nailed to a Cross that is most aptly described by His church as the Tree of Calvary. Horizontal trends, however, soon begin to emerge. In the Holy Supper, the flesh and the blood of Christ are prominent symbols; as such, perhaps, still spiritual, yet one may be forgiven for thinking that the mystery might have been conveyed by means of less animal images. One is reluctantly driven to the conclusion that this august and lofty moment of nascent Christianity reveals a conflict of spiritual and carnal, vertical and horizontal tendencies, which their symbolic value is unable to resolve. Communion, based as it is on transubstantiation, manifests a similar conflict. However subtle the arguments of learned theologians and shrewd psychologists aiming at an illustration and explanation of the mystical and symbolic values of Eucharist, the fact remains that as a religious practice among simple people Communion calls forth emotions and experiences of an insufficiently spiritual nature.

Do we have to recall the widespread, indeed universal adoption of the image, sheep–and–Shepherd by the Christian world? Or that the Supreme Victim is described as *Agnus Dei*? All the vertical urge that lives in Christianity—and it is indeed vigorous, as we are about to see—does not seem strong enough to repress the no less vigorous tendency of the Christian churches to express themselves in a language and in images of an obviously horizontal nature. That very esoterism which elevates and dignifies the mysteries of the Christian religion in its Catholic variety, and which seems to fascinate a certain type of over-strained intellectual, is itself a bivalent element—vertical for the selected few, horizontal for the sheep nourished with 'spiritual alfalfa'. In Catholicism, there lurks a domineering element that the crowd of sheep would not perhaps accept so meekly did they not find it in themselves as a reminiscence of their four-footed existence.

Even so, the vertical element prevails in the Cross. 'Love and femininity' is the message of the arms open in a horizontal; while the vertical expresses virility and a yearning for the All-Highest even beyond death. Death imposes a return to the horizontal even beyond the animal level, down to the physical; down to the wiping out of all differences, under the inexorable law of material inertness. The Cross, therefore, represents the triumph of life over death, of the unique over the common, of spirit over matter. Through the Cross, the Christian religion rises to the summit of the substance of religion, above all other forms or confessions.

If we now, from our specific point of view, endeavour to discriminate between the inner differences, the shadings, that distinguish the several forms of Christianity from each other, our judgment as to their varying degrees of verticality may be harder to come by. Since it stresses worship rather

71

than morality, the Catholic church might seem the most vertical. Of the two sets of human relations, with God and with other men, the Catholic church emphasizes the first, and even that which we owe to men is, in her doctrine, so due for love of God. This attitude is beautifully vertical.

Yet, bearing in mind how insistently the Reformed churches emphasize the need for a direct communication between the Christian and 'his' God, Protestantism would have a claim to be the more vertical of the two chief forms of Christianity. The constant intromission of the Catholic clergy between the Christian and God would appear to lower the faithful to the level of a flock (which they are often reminded they are).

Nevertheless, facing certain concrete dangers, the Catholic church has assumed a more vertical attitude than, at any rate, the Lutheran. Thus in resisting nazism. This fact might be better understood in the light of nationalism. Catholicism is an international, or rather supranational, faith. Lutheranism is a national and even a nationalistic religion, a transposition of the gregarious character of the Germans into the religious key. The peoples of Europe are nationalistic in inverse ratio to the strength of Roman Catholicism in them. This observation is two-edged. Spain, Italy, and to a lesser extent France are able to overcome their nationalism and to enter into a human, universal attitude more easily than nations of a Teutonic root, which are too arrogant to reach universality; but on the other side, they are looser in social sense and public discipline.

The most perfectly gregarious people in Europe is the English. That is why it has cut out a special religion to fit itself and no other people on earth, a kind of English suburb of Paradise, known as the English (i.e. Anglican) Church. The English still call it *the* Catholic church (the Catholic church proper being reduced to a local status as the *Roman* Catholic Church), thus disregarding, with a disarming indifference, the contradiction between 'catholic' (i.e. universal) and 'English'. The fact is that at bottom they do not see their religion as a slice cut off from the Catholic faith for their own home consumption, but rather as the Catholic religion proper, purified by the expulsion of all those foreigners.

# 4

The cow is now peacefully browsing the tiny leaves that grow at the root of the tree. She casts her eyes this way and that, and chooses and bites tentatively, and finally tears and cuts what she finds good. God knows why, the sight makes me think of a scientist at his research, and at first I find it hard to guess what the bridge can be between what I am seeing—the cow—and what I am imagining—the scientist. The explanation, though, turns up after a while. It was that word 'browse' which had done the trick; for it does mean both what the cow is doing on the meadow and what the scientist might be doing among his instruments and books.

Here we are again under that impression of indifference towards orientation which typifies the quadruped. The scientist, at the time unpolarized by any precise orientation, lets himself wander from here to there in his library—a meadow of books—or in his laboratory—a meadow of facts, and he himself calls it browsing, for he sees himself as a cow biting at twigs. Experience provided by chance proceeds from our horizontal past. It springs from the same root as empiricism, a wisdom accumulated seriatim that makes of Sancho Panza 'a bag of truths' lacking any cement of thought to unite them.

And we have already noted how, even after our vital levels have been decanted and separated by our assuming a vertical position, it is possible for the intellectual to live on his level in a horizontal and cowish way, browsing here and there on observable facts picked up without necessarily feeling in him that vertical impetus that would unify and organize them into a harmonic whole. I recollect having once visited a big astronomic centre in California in which, as my guide (a young American philosopher) put it to me, a number of technicians were capable of estimating from photographs the velocity of a galaxy almost at a glance and yet were unable to feel the slightest interest in the general scientific conclusions to be drawn from such an estimation. They were undoubtedly men in whom the horizontal tendency still prevailed over the vertical.

Both tendencies are at work in every endeavour towards knowledge, in every field. Some minds will rather seek the *how* of things; other minds, the *why*. The former will be the browsers, the horizontal ones, the cows; obeying no particular orientation, theory, or hypothesis, they will issue forth in search of a crop of facts. The latter will be the dreamers, the vertical ones, the trees; definitely polarized along some vertical thought, they will group and organize the facts and the data into a framework or fabric of general ideas that may unite them as a whole discernible from above.

It may well be, therefore, that the how–minds and the what–minds correspond to a deep, possibly ancestral difference. In history, for instance, the difference is patent between the data-compiler, whose work may be likened to that of the brick-maker and the bricklayer, and the architect who directs how the bricks are to be laid so that the building lives. A similar difference may be found in the field of pure science. In general, therefore, one may risk the opinion that for every branch of knowledge, the horizontal impulse hands on tradition, while the vertical impulse renews it. It is to the what– or why–minds that science owes its leaps forward; the how–minds just make it step along. Their glance does not rise above the level of their eyes. For each his meadow. How–minds tend to become specialized. What–scientists try to widen their field of observation as much as they can. This endeavour is becoming more ambitious and open to frustration, precisely because the work of crowds of specialists has proved so fertile in local and partial results; but when a vertical spirit achieves a view of the whole under a new light, every partial result may be transfigured. Newton, Planck, Einstein cause true revolutions in science.

Obviously both tendencies, the vertical and the horizontal, are at work in all scientists. It is a matter of mere dosage. The great discoverer, the pure vertical, is the mind that detects a new pattern in the facts. It seems (or so at any rate it is asserted by a Venezuelan observer) that when closely studied the vast, crowded scene painted by Michelangelo in the Sistine Chapel reveals colossal profiles of Jesus Christ and Dante. The idea would be wholly within the style of that great artist's imagination, both from the point of view of the pictorial *tour de force* and from that of its symbolic value. This type of discovery of a pattern that raises the meaning and the value of mere facts put together is not unlike the work of the vertical scientist.

We all remember the growing satisfaction of the man of the Newtonian era reaching towards an almost divine pride at the end of the nineteenth century. Planck's formula, which was to shatter it, became public in Berlin in December 1900. History can at times be astonishingly punctual. The twentieth century began in a mood so revolutionarily new that even Planck, the author of the change, stood more nonplussed than pleased at so much revolution. His theory of quanta had banished continuity, refuted the old tag about nature never leaping, and established that everything happens in packets—that there are no ramps, only flights of steps.

For the layman, it did not seem to matter very much. But in fact it did. Einstein made use of the new idea for a new study of light, representing it as an emission of packets or quanta of energy; the outcome of it being that physicists can only explain certain happenings, such as the luminous

76

radiations of metals, by conceiving light as composed of quanta or photons; while they can only explain other facts, such as interferential phenomena, by assuming that light is composed of waves. But we cannot afford to get lost in the labyrinthine avenues of modern physics. Let it be enough to say that after the field of physical thought had been ploughed by such men as Planck, Einstein, Becquerel, the Curies, Niels Bohr, Broglie, Schrödinger, and Heisenberg, physics had ceased to be an absolutely objective, exact, clear science, as neat a representation of material things and events as the nineteenth century had dreamt of and enjoyed, and had lost not only its clarity but its pride as an objective and exact form of knowledge. For it had discovered that the observed and the observer can no longer be kept apart.

The very bases of science undergo a change. The border line that Descartes had drawn between *res cogitans* and *res extensa* becomes blurred. Man, who on assuming a vertical posture had fancied that he was going to separate his intellect from things, the better to look at them, finds that there are two sets of happenings in nature—those that occur within volumes of very small dimensions or at very large velocities—which he is unable to observe without injecting a subjective factor into his calculations. And, as if this conclusion did not suffice, another and an even more disturbing one is forced upon his reluctant acquiescence: that it is impossible to attain an exact knowledge of *both* the emplacement and the velocity of a small physical particle. The more we know about the one the less we know about the other. This law of indetermination, formulated by Heisenberg, would appear to oppose an impassable barrier to human knowledge.

Nature has thus evaded, so far, the most determined and enlightened endeavours of man's intellect to pierce through to her secret; and this evasion is twofold. By subjecting observation not only to the object observed but also to the person who observes, nature in herself never appears before man. Man is only allowed to see nature as she is *when observed*. Science, therefore, does not reveal to man the objective essence of nature; but only a 'nature' which goes no further than that which man is capable of seeing in it.

The second way by which nature evades being caught in man's intellectual nets is Heisenberg's law of indetermination Thus far and no further, that law lays down; and so clearly that on the actual emplacement of this barrier of indetermination there is no indetermination whatsoever.

Of course, in a way, we knew it all. We knew that what we observe with our senses is a mere interpretation of the world that our senses hand on to us, determined as they are both by what they can and by what they cannot do. Were human eyes sensitive to frequencies higher than those of the violet or lower than those of the red lines of the spectrum the world would 'spread' into a wider range of colours than that we know. And a similar conclusion would go for our ear power. What we call the 'world' is therefore but one aspect, limited by our senses, of the real and effective world—whatever that may mean.

Let alone the fact that we might have been endowed with other senses beyond our imagination. Who knows how many more aspects of the world exist that, had we access to them, would fill us with joys similar to, or even deeper than, those we now owe to our sight and our hearing? The world of science is that which we see and hear and touch and taste and smell, slightly widened by scientific extrapolations that supply thought with raw material for calculations and hypotheses. What we are able to deduce from it all is that 'real nature' must be much vaster and richer in aspects than anything experience and science are able to reveal to us.

But there is more still—or should we say less? What happens this side of the barrier? In the present state of physical-science thought it is possible to determine the equation of probability of an event at a given time *t*, and also at another given time $t + 1$; but as to what happens between the two instants, the physicist declares himself nonplussed. And even so, in order to come to an agreement as to what goes on in nature or in their laboratories, on what it is exactly they are measuring, on the actual sense of their equations, physicists have not only had to create new concepts—which is quite natural—but also a new language —which is somewhat disquieting—and even a new logic—in which one may be pardoned for fearing a danger to the coherence and homogeneity of human thought. Thus, for instance, if I do not misinterpret Heisenberg: when there is a possibility that an electron may happen to be in one or the other of two communicating spaces in a laboratory, our day-to-day logic tells us that the observer will know that it is in one space or in the other, or that he does not know in which it is; but modern physics apparently requires yet a fourth logical posture, namely that the case is not solved; for to say that the observer does not know where the electron is amounts to a positive conclusion, or to 'taking sides'.

Note how humble and modest our modern physics is, which has nevertheless wrenched from nature the key to the nuclear powder-magazine, and bids fair to conquer the moon and the planets. The twofold revolution launched by Planck with his theory of quanta, and developed by Einstein with his theory of relativity, swept like a hurricane through the peaceful orchards of scientific thought. In 1923, while on a visit to Niels Bohr in his Copenhagen laboratory, I had a talk with this great mind, one of those who led that revolution, the effects of which are still being felt, for the dust it raised has not yet settled. The word he uttered most frequently was 'renunciation'. The scientist had to reconcile himself to renouncing complete knowledge of what was, in fact, unknowable. Next to renouncing, his most frequent word was 'complementarity'. Observations of space and of velocity were complementary. Representations of the atom as a system of particles and as a system of waves were

79

complementary. Calculations of physical events by Newton's laws or by Planck–Einstein laws were complementary. If now and then the one did not fit the other . . . , well, what of it?

Indetermination or determinism? Scientific objectivity or intervention of a subjective element? This science of our century subjects its adepts to cruel dilemmas. To begin with, that which in the nineteenth century had been considered as the sovereignty of physics, the fact that it was an exact and therefore unanimous science, has become blurred. No one in the nineteenth century dreamt of opposing Hippocrates to Galen as is done in medicine, which is more of an art than a science. But when one day in Geneva I asked Einstein what he thought of Bohr's ideas, he did not hide his dissent—as if both were not physicists but mere physicians, or even philosophers.

Einstein himself was by no means free from critics. Two of his most eminent adversaries emerged from the ever lively fields of French philosophy. Henri Bergson and Jacques Maritain raised concrete objections against some of his conclusions, in particular those that went beyond the bounds of strict physical science; and, at least with regard to Bergson, it must be owned that Einstein allowed himself to assume a disdainful attitude which his critic's outstanding intellect hardly justified. Bergson's criticisms have been restated vigorously by Ernest Ansermet.[1] A Spanish physicist and mathematician, a member of the Spanish Academy of Sciences, has published a number of technical statements in refutation of certain aspects of the theory of relativity as conceived by Einstein, precisely those which had caused Bergson's and Maritain's objections, i.e. the relativization of the notion of time and of the behaviour of the clock. Palacios is not an opponent of relativity; far from it: he puts forward equations to establish it on a

[1] Henri Bergson, *Durée et relativité*. Jacques Maritain, *Reflexions sur l'Intelligence*. Ernest Ansermet, *op. cit*. Julio Palacios, several pamphlets in Spanish and in English.

mathematical basis, free from Einstein's jugglings with the watch. It is not for me to decide who is right and who is wrong in this discussion between great minds; my purpose is just to point to the new climate of opinion which allows schools of thought within a science once believed to be exact.

Under the stress of this uneasiness, which so much doubt over the certainties of old aroused in their minds, some of the more afflicted scientists met in Copenhagen in 1926. By then the 'human' expression of the equations of Bohr was no longer the orbit of the electron, nor Schrödinger's wave of matter, but the wave of probability—a purely abstract concept inhabiting a multidimensional space. This is what Heisenberg wrote about these meetings:

> During the months following these discussions an intensive study of all questions concerning the interpretation of quantum theory in Copenhagen finally led to a complete and, as many physicists believe, satisfactory clarification of the situation. But it was not a solution which one could easily accept. I remember discussions with Bohr which went through many hours till very late at night and ended almost in despair; and when at the end of the discussion I went alone for a walk in the neighbouring park I repeated to myself again and again the question: Can nature possibly be as absurd as it seemed to us in these atomic experiments?[1]

Let us note again the contrast between the mood of this aggrieved confession of doubt and perplexity evinced by our contemporary physicists and the cocksure arrogance of those of the nineteenth century. They find they have to meet and discuss, even anxiously, in order to endeavour to come to an agreement on how to interpret their hypotheses, their concepts, and their calculations; and even so the 'clarifica-

[1] Werner Heisenberg, *Physics and Philosophy*.

tion' arrived at is only 'believed' 'satisfactory' by 'many physicists'. In other words, it is now possible to have an opinion, to believe, in matters pertaining to a once exact science. Furthermore, what is actually meant by 'absurd nature'? 'Nature' amounts to 'reality'—the sum total of objects and events, Descartes' *res extensa*. 'Absurd' amounts to 'rebellious to human reason', which may mean: either based on no reason or based on a reason other than human. We are, therefore, again confronted with that taut and hard dialogue between the creator of the Creator and the Creator of the creator. We don't seem able to agree. In order to reduce the Creator's world to the creator's reason, we have done all we could—making up concepts, reforming our language, stressing the limbs of our logic, and yet all we can present is a system of abstract equations that our intuition cannot manage to relate to what goes on.

These afflicted scientists are *what*-minds. Meanwhile, *how*-minds trot quietly on like a flock, their backs waving in the flow. The afflicted what–scientists are vertical, and as such they perhaps hope (possibly without realizing it) that facts and events will prove to be horizontal. Shepherds of physical facts and events, they seek a flock. They suffer because physical facts and events do not meekly obey in a horizontal flow the shouts of their self-appointed shepherd, who is trying to enclose them into a mathematical pen. We thus begin to adumbrate the possibility of a vertical nature that would refuse to let itself be bent into a horizontal posture. And this is no mere metaphor, as we shall see anon.

What is the outlook for an 'exact' science of nature? It does not seem that its progress is assured along the line that, beginning with Galileo, leads through Newton and Planck to Einstein and Heisenberg, a line bifurcating at the two last names. Nature bars the way with a sign of *lasciat' ogni speranza*, which this time reads: *indetermination complementarity*. If, therefore, it plods on along this path, its complexity is more likely to increase than its clarity. This conclusion is strengthened by the almost daily discoveries of new particles that turn the atom into a true world of events, births and deaths of sparks of energy–matter whose 'lives' vary from aeons or centuries to hours, minutes, seconds, or millionths of a second; in short, an inextricable world where but yesterday Niels Bohr had dreamt he saw a tiny solar system with its sun and its planets all in beautiful astronomic order.

All this is not merely astonishingly inextricable; it is also astonishingly inexplicable. It cannot be communicated to our common sense, to our imagination, or to our intuition. Science is nowadays less respected by the layman as science than held in awe as magic. Gadgets do work, bulbs do shed light on being switched on, the telephone does work (nearly always), the train does run, the computer does calculate. As science, though, it has emigrated to a limbo to which the layman, however intelligent, cannot follow it.

This might, nevertheless, contribute to raising the prestige of science among the masses. The power of the magician does not fall, rather does it increase, by the secret that clouds its actual causes. Let us recall the world-wide popularity Einstein attained overnight just because he had handed in at the Berlin Academy of Sciences a four page note that only a few thousand persons in the whole world were in a position to understand. Are we to assume that the multitude acclaimed him as a scientist, or as a magician? The multitude is herd-like, horizontal. They trust the shepherd and admire him because he is vertical. Medicine itself, even the most scientific, is essentially magic, in fact, faith-healing. The sick go to the doctor to be cured because they have faith in him; and his science, useful as it may be for him, has little other use for his patients than that of strengthening their faith. Science works as the religion of modern man, as his faith. And this faith consists in believing in the magic that we do not understand. That is why I pointed out at the time that, as happens now and then, chance had guessed accurately in naming *Einstein* the prophet of the new religion, for on that *stone* was the new Church to be erected.

This first perspective, then, the growth of a new science of physics on increasingly esoteric lines, need not imply a threat to the prestige of science with the masses; but it will weigh as a slab of lead on the mind of the scientist himself. That is why it may well happen that some day a great 'vertical' mind will clarify scientific thought by means of a revolution in its basic concepts. Who knows? Perhaps the trouble is due to the fact that the present stock of concepts—mass, force, momentum, velocity and the like—do not lend themselves to a picture that satisfies our intuition and commonsense; while another set of concepts might.

On the other hand, it is worth noting that this stony, dusty, and winding road which science has been painfully treading for sixty years has led it to a system built on the two notions of statistics and probability. The equations our modern physicists work on and with do not represent sparks or spots of energy or waves of matter but waves of probability based on calculations of statistics. And this is indeed food for thought; for it turns out that in his search for the true face of reality man finds a mask built up with our two typical notions, horizontal and vertical. Statistics, the science of indistinct and indifferent facts, is the lore of the herd; probability, the measure and scale of the exception, is the science of the unique. The former is the science of passive events; the latter is the study of the unlikely or not very likely—in other words, of original events. The former is the counting of heads of the cow-facts; the latter is the expectation of the facts that 'tree' themselves. Horizontal, vertical.

During one of my first talks with Einstein I asked him what he thought of determinism. The moment could not have been less propitious, for it happened during a reception offered in Geneva by an international institute of education I led at the time. 'Indetermination', he answered, 'is but the

84

measure of our ignorance. When we know more, determinism will return.' He spoke with complete confidence. 'But, Heisenberg?' I asked. Einstein was beginning to answer, and he was looking at me with his unforgettable eyes flooded with the light of perpetual wonder, when an old woman intervened and holding out her hand to him exclaimed in a squeaky voice: 'A cat may well look at a king.'

Einstein smiled at her as he might have smiled at the moon, showing in his puzzled features that he had no idea whatsoever of what she meant; he glanced at me again with his usual wonder, this time tinted with panic, and walked away dreaming God knows what across the crowd who bathed him in admiration. I stayed behind, thinking that no event less deterministic could have been imagined than that meeting, that question, that answer, that second question . . . and that apparition of the old woman with a cat in one hand and a king in the other . . .

But what self-confidence in Einstein—and under the self-confidence, what prejudice!

This is perhaps one of the most paradoxical constants of modern intellectual life: prejudice even in those who think themselves the freest of the free. All happens as if the horizontal forces—the ancestral cows—sooner or later managed to impress their law on to the vertical force—the ancestral tree—even in the most objective human field, which is that of science. Modern men have so often boasted of having risen above those intellectual limitations which loomed so large in the lives of Copernicus and Galileo that they may not realize to what an extent they still hold sway even in the world of modern science.

It may be argued that there are no Galileos in our day, grinding their teeth under the authority of modern inquisitors. But is that really so? In 1950, Immanuel Velikovsky put forward a system of propositions including the following:

1. The physical sequence of the world has not been peaceable and smooth, as tacitly or explicitly assumed since Newton, but on the contrary, scanned by cosmic catastrophes, some of which, as their traces prove, happened in historical times.

2. Insofar as the earth is concerned, the most important and most active agents of these catastrophes have been Mars and Venus.

3. Venus was a comet and became a planet as the outcome of one of these catastrophes.

4. The rotation of the earth was changed thereby: its period passed from 360 to 365'24 days; its direction from one way to the opposite, for in the previous era the sun rose in the West.

5. As a consequence, a historical mix-up has caused either a deficit of five hundred years in classical Hebraic chronology or a corresponding excess in the Egyptian. Velikovsky shows that it is the second alternative which fits the facts.

I should be unduly deforming this swift essay were I to enter into a detailed description of the episodes (well nigh incredible, some of them) of the odyssey of this vertical spirit resisting singlehanded, the onslaught of a herd of horizontal how–scientists, cows' horns down against a tree. Enough to state: that he was refused every opportunity to verify or refute his propositions by means of experiments which he suggested; that his book was the object of an incredible persecution even before it was published and, when published, before it was read; that his New York publisher, under threats he happened to be unable to disregard, had to request the author to give up his agreement at a time when the book was selling at the rate of a thousand copies a day; that Velikovsky was accused of scientific and historical errors he had not dreamt of committing, and that it was even said of him that he degraded science and religion.

Now, along with his propositions Velikovsky had put

into his adversaries' hands a number of scientific and historical hostages. One or two examples may help to add concreteness to this story. He asserted that, contrary to scientific tradition as it stood at the time (1950), celestial bodies possess electrical fields, and therefore, magnetic forces are an important element in celestial mechanics. This idea was then considered a scientific heresy. It is now embodied in official astronomy, with no mention of the first man who uttered it. He asserted that as a late planet Venus must show a very high temperature and be wrapped in an atmosphere of hydrocarbons, and that its rotation must be anomalous within the solar system. Bishops and cardinals there were in the scientific church who laughed at him. But in 1961 official radio-astronomic observations made in the United States revealed the temperature of Venus to be at least 300° C.; a year later the missile Mariner II, launched by the United States' space organization, put it at least 800° C. Velikovsky's assertion, made twelve years earlier, was thus vindicated, but only a small group of bold men in Princeton mentioned the name of the pioneer.

Finally, Goldstein's and Carpenter's radar observations (1962) proved that Venus gyrates 'the wrong way round' and very slowly—a fact that, after twelve years of its being adumbrated by Velikovsky, came to be discovered and interpreted as he had himself suggested. But again the name of yesterday's heretic was silenced by those who had belatedly opened the gates of official orthodoxy to his ideas. As for the atmosphere of hydrocarbons that surrounds Venus, it is now a scientifically accepted fact; but again no one gives a thought to the man who first put it forward. The vertical one is still unacceptable to the herd of horizontals who feed in the official stalls, in spite of the fact that no one has so far been able to suggest a complete theory capable of explaining all these facts—except Velikovsky.

Even so, it might be argued, science as such is not ostracized today. There is no pariah science. Well, there is. More than a century has gone by since Hahnemann wrote, and homeopathy is still ostracized, still waiting at the gates of medical schools, looked down upon as hardly better than quackery. Parapsychology is hardly beginning to be considered as respectable. Those with long memories and ages still remember how hard it was for Pasteur, a mere veterinary to persuade doctors of medicine to let him hold an opinion of his own, and how a famous Parisian doctor showed his bovine disdain for that 'veterinary's' ideas by letting his lancet deliberately fall to the (then dusty) floor of his operating theatre, happy to let his patients die rather than recognize that Pasteur was right.

I have already referred to the case of Julio Palacios and his opposition to certain aspects of Einstein's relativity theories. Though not altogether illiterate in such matters, I do not feel competent enough even to offer my views—let alone decide who is right, he or Einstein. I am able to say that Julio Palacios is an original and capable mathematical physicist, whose *Dimensional Analysis* is respected throughout the world as a contribution to modern science; and that his theory has so far been refuted by no one; and yet he is unable to have it published in official reviews (save Spanish ones) because it does not conform to orthodox views.

All this digression may perhaps excuse me for having found singularly prejudiced the confident and professional answer Einstein gave me when I asked him what he thought of determinism. Before a situation, to say the least, doubtful, Einstein believed (and even, it seemed, hoped) that determinism would again prevail. He had, in fact, taken sides. It is generally assumed that a scientist is an impartial observer of nature out of the virgin forest of facts, who endeavours to disentangle a pattern, a general trend, a 'habit', which he will then decorate with the name of 'law'. What does actually happen?

It may happen that the observer imagines he has discovered such a pattern and then acquires a vested interest in his discovery which, even if in the end it will fit the ways of nature he has been observing, may not necessarily be identical with these ways and their inner essence. At the next turning of the road of his enquiry, he may in fact find that the coincidence has ceased which had so far united nature and pattern. Henri Poincaré used to say that if tomorrow the sun did not rise the laws of astronomy would have to be revised. When I was a student at the Ecole Polytechnique (and of Poincaré, who was a professor in it) an 'examiner' in astronomy had put together an equation which he thought ruled the oscillations of the students' marks round the axis of the average. His colleagues were not slow in perceiving curious discrepancies between this examiner's estimates of our capacity and application and theirs, whereby it soon became evident that the happy discoverer wittingly or unwittingly raised or lowered his marks so as to fit his equation. It cost him his post.

An extreme case, to be sure, yet a symbolic one. It would be hardly an exaggeration to say that all science is nowadays evolving under the sway of a subtle and tacit prejudice or prepossession which might be defined thus: *Everything in the universe can be or will eventually be reduced to physio–chemical laws in their turn capable of being turned into mechanical laws in their turn formulable by mathematical laws*. Up to a point this prejudice (which inspired Einstein's answer to me) is functional in the scientist—a kind of professional deformation of his mind. The field of science is that which admits of measure. Where there is no measuring there is no science. Science, moreover, carries within its nature the duty to extend its sway without limit. Therefore, the prejudice just defined is not only natural to science, it is part of its very nature.

We are not, therefore, criticising or censuring the mechanist and determinist (a generation ago, we would have written 'materialist') prejudice which dominates science. It is where it should be, and it fulfils its purpose. All we are after is: first, to refuse to bow to this prejudice (or to its contrary) when it is not needed for applying the mind directly to problems subtler than those that admit of measure; and secondly, within the framework of this disquisition, to point out how 'cow-like, how horizontal, that prejudice is. It is typical of the research herd, of the how–scientists. It is transmitted through a horizontal tradition. It creates a mass, a push, an atmosphere; and it can roll over any vertical, why–mind not served by strong enough powers of will.

When from physics we pass to biology the mechanicist prepossession of the man of science seems to become sharper. The biologist is well aware of the fact that his field of observation is both very similar to, and very different from, that of the physicist. Nothing more tempting and even, up to a point, more fecund, than to see in the skeleton the creation of a Leonardo of mechanics. There occur, more-over, in organisms a not inconsiderable number of events that are best described in physical or chemical terms. From which observation only a step leads to considering organisms as 'systems' subject to physical and chemical laws. That step is the golden dream of many—possibly most—biologists. That is exactly where their prejudice is at work.

These mechanist biologists look upon themselves as more modern and free thinking than the 'vitalists'. One of their features is their staunch obstinacy in extending to organisms the second law of thermodynamics. A noble endeavour, by all means, to which we owe works of a considerable scientific interest.[1] The most admirable aspect of these works is the very determination, the vigour of the prejudice, which drives the authors to set in motion their utmost ingeniousness in order to compel vital events to

[1] Such as *Time's Arrow of Evolution* by H. F. Blum. Princeton, 1955.

re-enter the mechanical world as a living body forced into a Procrustian bed. It is a curious case of faithful infidelity or of faithless fidelity to science; for this obstinate endeavour to reduce biology to a mere branch of physics tends to deprive the scientist of his impartiality.[1]

That the second law of thermodynamics may work in the case of some well defined cycles of events *within* living organisms, if they can be considered in sufficient isolation and proved to be ruled by physical laws, would appear to be not only correct but rather tautological; but that the law can rule the organism itself is an assertion that would be hard to substantiate. There are a number of reasons in the way. The first is the fact that the second law of thermodynamics applies only to closed systems, and organisms are always open systems. Organisms are systems endowed with a *sui generis* unity we call 'vital', a unity characterized by two features: every part of it presupposes the whole and can only be understood as such a part of such a whole; and the inner whole depends on the outer whole, including air, sea, earth, and sun. One might well define an organism as a *centre of world functional perspective*. To isolate it amounts to killing it. An organism, therefore, cannot obey the second law of thermodynamics.

If, following the modern trend, we are to understand the second law of thermodynamics as a statistical law, which enjoins on every system a change from more order to less order, from less probability to more probability, then *every* organism belies this law. Without a human (or purposeful animal) intervention, things are more likely to decay than to rise in the scale of order. Left to themselves, a house, a wall, a heap of stones, will go on decaying (i.e. *falling*, seeking the horizontal) because their parts will submit to the higher probability. While an organism seeks the unlikely.

[1] This reduction of the scope of biology may well be compared to the arguments of a veterinary surgeon that medicine is a branch of veterinary science on the ground that man is but a part of the animal kingdom.

A fly is a most unlikely arrangement of molecules. A human brain far more so. And the human brain has no sense but as the central organ of the whole man. So, though under the pressure of scientific prejudice the reverse is often asserted, it is obvious that life contradicts or evades the second law of thermodynamics, and moves from the more probable to the less probable and even to the unique.

Furthermore, organisms transcend the physical world. We are getting into trouble here; for physicists may argue that this assertion is a *petitio principii*. Nor would they be altogether wrong. But if we reveal bad news to a sensitive person, this fact can on no account be described as physical; and yet that person will experience effects which can be so described. The life of organisms rests on an intercommunication between the physical and the nonphysical that recalls osmosis, but an osmosis between two different worlds. An organism therefore reaches beyond the physical. This aspect, which is typical of at any rate the higher forms of organic life, attains its fullest expression, of course, in man; but it can also be observed in animals. Organisms are, therefore, systems open not only to outer physical forces, which would be enough to free them from the second law of thermodynamics, but also to happenings outside and beyond the field of physics; which proves that the persistence in reducing them to obeying the second law of thermodynamics is purely irrational.

It is a gregarious and horizontal persistence which proved irresistible even for such eminently vertical men as Einstein and Planck. In a fascinating booklet, *What is Life?* Schrödinger explains that food is a means whereby organisms seek to counteract the tendency of entropy towards its maximum or, in other words, to remedy the natural tendency of the organism to decay. He does not, however, seem to be aware of the relevance for his argument of this important fact: that living organisms can only feed on live matter or on substances derived from it. When a physical system has to be provided with more energy (i.e. deprived of some entropy) it is fed with air, fuel, or both. But our body must be given meat or bread; vegetables need a land rich in living micro-organisms. It does not seem reasonable, therefore, to present nutrition as a thermodynamical fact. Yet the prepossession persists.

There was a time when thermodynamics tyrannized over the field of food to such a degree that human diet was practically reduced to a figure of calories. Even in our day, a scale of calories is often found convenient to compare if not to measure diets; but at least in our time it is realized that such a thermic measurement is not sufficient, and that factors outside such an equation between heat and energy must be brought in—the so-called vitamins. The discovery of vitamins amounted to a revolution in our ideas about food. This revolution consisted in the reincorporation into the system of the criterion of *quality*. Reincorporation, because this criterion of quality in matters of food had always been tacitly if not expressly acknowledged by everybody before the thermodynamic prepossession of scientists had all but expelled it from at any rate the thoughts of dietitians, if not the instinct of housewives. But what sort of energy is this, which vitamins bring to the body, indispensable to its life yet only in minute quantities?

We are thus thrown back on to the same theme: quantity, i.e. uniformity, herd, horizontal, cow; versus quality, uniqueness, individual, vertical, tree.

There is another functional prejudice in the biologists, which negates the finality, the purpose, the intelligent direction of evolution in organisms. That marvel, the human eye, is for them the outcome of pure chance working through millions of years; a lucky stroke of dice produced the heavy molecule of protein; and so, in the course of the ages, from luck to luck, 'nature' 'evolved' that astonishing instrument the human brain and its no less astonishing appendages, eyes, ears, and other sense organs. An obvious

93

prejudice, even though apt and useful from the point of view of the development of science itself. But why should we submit to it, all those of us whose function does not happen to be the subjection (insofar as it is possible) of all vital facts to some measuring tape?

It was no doubt a worthwhile and praiseworthy work that emancipated the sciences of nature from the ideas and the language that subordinated them more than was strictly necessary to an inscrutable and unmeasurable source of power such as divine will, or anything smacking of divine intention or will in any shape or form. But it can be seriously asserted that modern biology is altogether free from similar tendencies? Or should we rather recall here the famous French classic:

*Chassez le naturel, il revient au galop.*

The fashion nowadays will require that a number of life happenings be explained by means of an undoubtedly ambiguous concept: *information*. Genes, for instance, in the design of their proteins, carry we are told, the 'information' needed for the organism to develop and become an oak, a frog, or an elephant. May a layman point out that the word 'information' is utterly meaningless unless it implies *intention* and therefore *will*? Who is that mysterious being who is endowed with a will to wish to inform another entity, and with intelligence enough to invent a code to convey the message in a language common to the informing and to the informed ones? And how is one to harmonize this attitude with the mechanical or physico–chemical view of biology?

A similar prejudice, leading to similar irrational attitudes, inspires the (otherwise useful) laboratory endeavours to achieve the synthesis of certain organic substances, such as proteins and even cells. Praiseworthy in themselves, they will appear as less praiseworthy if they are looked upon, as they often are, as steps forward towards the definition of life as a set of physico-chemical phenomena. Nothing can come out of a laboratory that does not proceed from man, who is life; so that a laboratory-made compound is not physical but vital. And the same goes for electronic computers, 'brains', 'translators', and other similar wonders—all emanations of the human mind.

It may be argued that if we did achieve the laboratory synthesis of a protein, proof would have been given of the possibility of life having begun on our planet by sheer chance; since, though the likelihood of it would be very small, the amount of time would be very great. This argument is not sound. On the one hand, it is not one but many radically different molecules that would be needed, so that the unlikelihood of spontaneous life is astronomically high; on the other, time is not so very long. Velikovsky has shown that the life of suns and planets does not flow in a kind of semi-eternal tranquility, for it is cut by cosmic catastrophes. Evolution does not have at its disposal an unlimited amount of time. And, in any case, the argument reveals to what extremes scientific prejudice is apt to resort. It is surely more natural to think that the very high degree of unlikelihood inherent in organisms, and above all in man, is not due to a blind, horizontal force stretched throughout the aeons, but to the free and purposeful impulse of a vertical Creator.

As for the so-called social sciences: it might even be found easier still to analyse the vertical and the horizontal components in this field, for sociology is composed of elements the study of which is best approached either through psychology or through statistics, and our first intuition will award a vertical value to the former and a horizontal value to the latter. A tempting parallel between sociology and physics will suggest itself here; one which recalls Niels Bohr's favourite idea of complementarity. Waves or electrons? the physicists asked themselves. And Niels Bohr answered: 'Waves for one aspect of things and electrons for the other'. To which, Heisenberg added: 'The more we shall know about waves the less we shall know about electrons'. But both conclude: 'The one and the other approach are equally necessary for the understanding of the facts'.

Now, there is a family air between this way of looking at physical phenomena and the methods which the mere observation of social happenings recommends to the sociologist; for individual facts are better approached through psychology, and collective facts through statistics; the former belong to the vertical, the latter to the horizontal, style of life. Facts considered in their mass admit of a statistical study—which, of course, does not penetrate much into the arcana of individual behaviour; while individual facts lend themselves to a psychological approach that, in its turn, is of little use for conclusions on mass behaviour. And yet, for an adequate knowledge of human societies, both avenues are necessary and neither is sufficient. The tree and the cow elements act separately, but knowledge of both types of action is indispensable to an awareness of what actually goes on.

Of course, statistics will tend towards determinism; but it seems that psychology should not permit the slightest doubt about its being the science of vertical events. This, however, is not a popular view nowadays, particularly in the United States where, to judge by the intransigent rationalism often to be found there, the gregarious, horizontal type of sociologist may well predominate. The United States has given the world a prodigious example of political and social stability. This success might well be due to the prevalence among Americans of a horizontal, gregarious tendency which endows them with an easy inward slope towards conformism. What the Communist Party has been trying hard for generations to force upon the people of Russia, the people of the United States have

96

achieved spontaneously. All feel the same, and the few who do not, try to adapt themselves to the general feeling.

It was therefore to be expected that the studies which illustrate the socializing action of the collective environment on the thoughts, feelings, and language of men should flourish in such a country. It is obvious that the circumstances in which a man lives powerfully contribute to modelling the figure that he will be taking on in the course of time; but this action of circumstances can hardly ever come to be a determining factor of the personality, or even a contributing factor in the same degree for all. If, for instance, we compare a hundred Englishmen or Americans who have spent twenty years abroad, there is sure to be a certain trace of the influence of their foreign abodes in all of them; yet no two will be found—even among those whose life abroad has been most similar—in whom such an influence has produced identical results in quality or in quantity. Furthermore, this action of the foreign herd is sure to be stronger on horizontal than on vertical types.

This observation may help us to look on with a sense of proportion and some optimism at the threats of all kinds which our present world raises against individual liberty. At most, these threats might actually become a danger for Anglo-Saxon and Teutonic peoples; less so for others. Yes, it is true, modern societies are growing more and more mechanized; yes, more and more the average man receives an ever increasing number of radio and television impressions that condition and even determine him; a multitude of social impacts come to beat the individual soul like a piece of copper at the hands of the artificer, and to give it a predetermined shape. All this is true. But all this is ephemeral.

We are living in an epoch such as mankind has never known. Horizontal forces exert an exceptional pressure on vertical ones. The number of persons rises; their uprooting grows apace, as well as their concentration into areas of high human density that must perforce be served by collective and uniform means. Everywhere quantity–horizontal overrides quality–vertical. The statistical, definitely horizontal, and gregarious forms of present-day demagogical democracy all work in the same direction. The essential problem at the core of the political organization of nations is not solved. This problem may be defined as the *contriving of ways whereby to elect the aptest for government*. This problem cannot be—shall we say *solved*—that would be too ambitious too soon—cannot be properly tackled save by institutions objectively adequate. But these vertical aims are countered by the innate tendency of the masses to let themselves go to the horizontal, to be a herd.

The difference between a mass and a people consists in this: that a mass has no institutions. A people left without institutions becomes a mass, a herd. There is a strong vertical element in a people rich in institutions, none in a mass, which is horizontal. Modern democracy has gone astray in that it has based its faith on the dogma of direct universal suffrage. *Suffrage* is all right. *Universal* is all right. But *direct* is a disaster because it does not allow any space for institutions between the mass and the elect; so that the mass is thus prevented from developing into a people, from achieving *verticality*. It remains a herd. That is perhaps why it soon grows bored with elections, a trend countered by the compulsory vote, an absurd paradox whereby the citizen is deprived of his sovereignty in order to force him to exert it.

This disastrous, direct-vote system is purely statistical, i.e. horizontal, less than animal, mechanical. Democracy can only be saved if it *organizes* itself, or, in other words, if it forsakes quantity–disorder for quality–order. And as it shows no signs of entering this path of salvation, politics comes to add one more factor to the many that in our day help to favour quantity against quality. Two sources of hope remain, however: the necessity of a liberating evolution, and its possibility.

That necessity is rooted in man's very essence. Even in the countries that strike us as most gregarious and horizontal man is essentially vertical. The quadruped in him 'treed' himself one day, whether *motu proprio* or by an inspiration from 'the Highest' does not matter much here. The fact is that he treed himself. He can hardly have done it to let himself later be untreed or cowed by circumstances. The more so as circumstances are mostly of his own making. It seems, therefore, natural to think that, threatened by modern developments with a return to the animal status, he will know how to *stand up* to the threat.

As for the possibility of freeing himself from such circumstances, there is no doubt that it exists. He who was able to rise above his first, natural animality will be able to rise against his second, social one. That much is forecast by the very forms of the social mechanics which are now enslaving him; for these forms are becoming every day more flexible and more open to an evolution favourable to freedom. At bottom, the power motive that drives technical progress is an urge for more freedom. It matters little, in a long-term perspective (much as it may in a short-term view), that its first effect (or, rather, its second) may be contrary to its end. For instance, the first effect of the invention of the mechanical carriage was an increase in freedom, since thousands were emancipated from the tyranny of the railway—a rigid, collective, 'horizontal' system of transport; but its second effect was regressive and contrary to freedom, for mass production and circulation of cars has all but cancelled their advantages. The social pressure that caused the trouble will have to contrive its remedy.

In the end, our optimism rises from a faith it seems reasonable enough to hold in the vigour of man's vertical urge. This vertical urge it is that constitutes the essence of liberalism. Once a man has 'treed' himself, he will not consent to be 'untreed'. The whole emancipating movement that modern history records in men and nations amounts

99

to the 'treeing' of beings that were once in an inner horizontal position. This movement becomes deeper and swifter in the modern world, but its origins go back to antiquity. Liberty is already a magic word in Cicero. And liberty is the spiritual foliage of the Tree of the Cross.

# 5

---

I have sat a long while contemplating the beauty of the tree while the cow, sitting on the grass, ruminates placidly. And I start thinking that there is no placidity about the tree. Of course, there are trees and trees in the arboreal people. The cedar seems to be advising calm, while I have seen oaks which seem to be . . .

Angrily shooting upwards out of an ardent earth.

In the tree, the trunk and the branches appeal to us as prefigurations of the body and arms of man. A line or two of Victor Hugo come to mind over those two trees . . .

*qui font des gestes dans le vent*
*comme deux avocats qui parlent pour et contre.*

The image is vivid enough; yet I do believe the poet went astray in choosing to depict his two trees actually moving physically, when what characterizes the tree, what makes it a premonition, a prophecy of man, is its merely esthetical movement—the suggestion of motion while remaining motionless. Yes, there are trees whose 'gestures' recall the barrister, or the grandfather, or the priest, or the mystic . . . but the marvel of it all is that they are *motionless* gestures, which convey the sense of movement without moving.

Its hour will come for an exploration of the avenues which this marvel opens to our thought and imagination. For the present, let us glance at the marvel itself. On the one hand, the placidity of the mobile cow; on the other, the vivacity of the motionless tree. This contrast, this union between essential movement and physical immobility, is perhaps the secret of the tree's beauty; of that attractiveness in it which makes us look at it and look at it again and never cease to enjoy looking at it.

It rises from the ground in a straight vertical, as an offering to the All–Highest, with a gesture that sums up and sublimates all its other motionless gestures. These are of various styles, according to the species; but the motionless gesture which sublimates them all is ever the same: one of offering— an impression due to the vertical urge of all trees, even those which, like the willow, seem to seek the earth with their foliage. Beholding them, man feels a fraternity towards them, rooted in a common vertical longing, so that the sight of a stem and foliage always makes him raise his eyes to heaven.

Powerful claws gripping the earth; sinewy trunk solitary rising; arms raised as if calling to heaven; all this muscular life, which moves without moving, speaks without words to the man who looks at it; and it seems to say to him that life is only found when it is not sought, and only reveals itself when one does not endeavour to understand.

The cow goes on ruminating, and the tree goes on calling to heaven—which very high, very high, remains silent. What beauty! Yet another mystery. What can beauty really be? So evident and so mysterious. A gift that draws us to its possessor and unites us with the beautiful in an ineffable joy. So joy and union would be the two attributes of beauty. But joy: what is it? Another mystery. Everyone can live it; no one knows what it is. The satisfaction of living deeply. Could it be that joy and union are but two aspects of the same vital pulsation?

Were it so, should we not have discovered a way of access to nature that mere science had found closed? Beauty expects love. Love is joy and union. This union is what we seek in vain with our head. We forget that our head has been separated from the rest of the body by the length of our neck. How can we unite our brain with any creature of this world when it is only a part of us? If we are to unite with some creature of the world, we must first become a complete and *single* creature ourself. In order to attain to that union which is knowing, it would therefore be necessary to re-unite in us what the vertical posture had separated; to remelt together brain and heart, to fecundate thought with feeling; to remake the whole man.

But then, a return to the horizontal? To the animal? To the cow? No. Because the perception of beauty is already a human experience that presupposes the vertical stand. What is required is a giving up of intellectual initiative, of the acquisitive will of the intellect. To comprehend is to apprehend, to *grasp*. Such had been our intention along the road of science. Reality, of course, evades our grasp. But let us renounce holding sway over it. Let us just behold it and enjoy its beauty, and that union we had wished to force it into will flourish of its own in mutual freedom.

This may perhaps be the deeper meaning of that delightful Gallegan proverb: *O que mais mira menos ve.* He who looks most sees least. The mere scientist looks too much; and on the other hand he *is* not enough. In order to look at things in his peculiar way—the surveyor's—he had to mutilate himself. The poet and the artist will look in a different way; not to conquer but to be conquered, and not with their mere intellects but with all the levels of their beings, gathered together and united at that of emotion.

Here, therefore, a vertical force of considerable power will be needed; for great art is vertical. A force capable of gathering together all the planes to concentrate them into an intelligent emotion. This vertical force, rising from the deepest self to intuition through the intellect to return thereby enriched to the *motive emotion* (if the pleonasm be allowed), is what is known as genius.

Nor does the word go here in its popular sense, somewhat

vague and undefined, nor in yet another one, more or less semi-popular, a mere superlative meaning a very big talent. As here understood, talent and genius differ in quality rather than in quantity. They are the two creative forces in all art. Genius is vertical; talent, horizontal. Genius is masculine and provides the fecundating instant—what is known as inspiration. Buffon's definition, 'a long patience' is a typically French error; for France, the richest country in the world in talent, not outstanding in genius. Talent is feminine, and given time and patience it develops and shapes the seed it received from genius. Paul Valéry's *Génie, oh longue impatience* does but reveal the relative shortness of his genius and the secret of his astonishing, nearly perfect talent. The relentless emphasis with which French criticism insists on form is the outcome of this predominance of talent over genius in the French character. The mistress of all in matters of talent, France gives forth a genius but rarely.

There is a story about Picasso that sheds some light on all this. He was eating in some *bistro* or other when he suddenly lifted his fork from his plate and glanced with a mischievous eye at a long hair hanging from it. '*Tiens, un Matisse!*' Whether it happened or not, the story is an eye-opener for the relation between French and Spanish creation. Picasso is an incomparable genius served by a talent which, though still formidable, is much more modest. That is why his art is astounding for the swiftness and self-confidence of its strategy, but also remarkable for the waywardness of its tactics. The very versatility of his styles is due not merely to the vigour of his genius but also to a certain, at any rate, relative indigence of his talent. The masculine, fecundating idea is strong, the feminine gestation not always worthy of it. Now, genius provides the strength of what the artist says, but the style comes from his talent. France is a country of more style than strength; Spain, of more strength than style. Goya fathered the whole of the French nineteenth century; Picasso, the twentieth.

In Spain, Unamuno is a genius with but little talent; Ortega a talent with but little genius. The finest talents in Spain were perhaps Garcilaso in letters and Velázquez in the arts, though even in them genius excelled talent. The reason why, even now, the French don't quite assimilate Shakespeare (as shown by Gide's translation of *Hamlet*), while he fascinates us Spaniards, is that Shakespeare is the most vigorous poetic genius Europe has given forth, and for us Spaniards what counts most is genius.

The Frenchman expects the work of art to present *du fini*, *du poli*. His talent recalls a well-furnished, well-ordered, clean, and neat house in which genius must 'behave' so as not to spoil the furniture or soil the carpets. Try to give those admonitions to Shakespeare or Dostoyevsky, to Goya or to Picasso. The geniuses that spring from our soils break walls, burst doors open, and dislocate forms with no respect for order, clarity, logic, or symmetry.

All this is, to be sure, a matter of more or less. It would be as silly to deny genius to France as talent to England or Spain. There is everything everywhere. The capricious wand of memory recalls here those two Frenchman of genius, so different from each other by the way, Rabelais and Pascal. Nor is it mere hazard that Valéry detested Pascal; for he was a typical nineteenth-century man who had lingered into the twentieth. 'For me', he once said to me in my house in Geneva, 'nothing exists but what comes through my senses'. And yet God knows how freely he was able to interpret what came to his senses by means of the all but perfect talent and the limited but penetrating genius that shone in his grey eyes. Today, France has given the world an eminently vertical genius in St. John Perse.

Among French classics, Corneille was more of a genius, Racine more of a talent; Molière more balanced between the two. A similar parallel might be made between Dostoyevsky, richer in genius than in talent, Turgeniev, richer in talent than in genius, and Tolstoi, more balanced. In

Europe, the greatest, most balanced creators may well be Leonardo, Bach, Mozart and Velázquez. Of Beethoven's quartets, there shines more talent in the first and more genius in the last; while the most balanced would be the three Rasumovsky and the three next (ten to twelve). In Shakespeare, genius overflows like an inebriateness which drives talent to impotence, so that even form becomes 'vertical' and genius-like, and images trip on each other, run over each other, and form becomes dynamic, in the manner of the form of a torrent. Something similar happens to Michelangelo.

Forms of human life, the arts also depend on what enters through the senses, whether they hold sway over space or over time. Space and time are the two coordinates of our life. The plastic arts deal with space; poetry and music with time. But it is as well to emphasize from the outset that these arts, as well as those which are born of their combination, meet in the same vital experience which is the union between the living being and the lived moment. The core of an art which has achieved its purpose is that inkling of eternity, that synthesis of eternity and time which man can only know in nature, and this only through art. Art is the only way to knowledge.

Like every thing alive, the work of art is a mystery. We would have it possess unity, but not that merely formal unity of the three rules of Aristotle or of Piero de la Francesca's perspective. Rather are we thinking of that essential unity which springs from the state of mind of the artist. What is required is an emotion in quantity and in quality, a state of mind that is definite, original, and real, resembling no other.

We also require that this state of mind be transferred to the canvas or the poem so that the spectator or reader receives it alive and re-creates it in his being. Where there is no emotion, there is no *work*. Where there is no transfer, there is no *art*.

How many sensitive souls there are and have been who beholding a sunset, a remembrance, a longing, have felt an emotion which, had they but been able to pass it on in all its original freshness, would have been acclaimed a work of art! But this work of art will not be born; and that initial emotion will gradually, slowly die in the inner individual silence like a sunset in the desert that no one will have feasted his eyes on. What was missing? Art. The capacity to mould the emotion into some material medium that will make it transmissible. *Art is therefore the faculty to master a certain order of matter in order to submit it to the service of the spirit.* Thus defined, art goes beyond the mere service of beauty. We speak of the art of persuading, and even of cooking.

Artists differ according to the material medium they can rule. Those princes of art that we owe to the golden era of Italy—Leonardo, Michelangelo—ruled over nearly every form of matter, and they were poets, painters, sculptors, and even musicians. Such versatility is rare nowadays. Picasso is perhaps the only name that comes to mind. Yet a sign that the artistic faculty as such may be a gift independent of the medium it masters to come through may be seen in the fact that artists in different media do often occur in families.

Some arts need more matter than others. From the more 'material' to the less, the scale might be: architecture, sculpture, painting, literature, music. It may seem strange to some that literature comes here before music, when the bulk of the instruments of an orchestra are borne in mind. But a theatre establishment is no less bulky than an orchestral whole, and the meaning of 'matter' in this context is different. We are not thinking of the weight and volume of the physical material that in an ancillary way serves this or that art; but of the weight and volume in which it manifests itself. In architecture, this matter is the whole edifice; in sculpture, bronze or marble; in picture, canvas and colours.

But as we pass from the arts of space to those of time the standard seems to draw within. The matter of literature is a system of concepts and words; that of music, a system of sounds.

*De la musique avant toute chose*, decreed Verlaine, with the shrewdness of a poet. Music is the soul of all arts. Harmony, melody, and rhythm are such intimate elements of esthetic emotion that they seem to be needed in every work of any art for man to be able to enjoy it. Music, moreover, is a sublimation of active life—the pure spirit of action rising to heaven when action itself is already dead. While in a state of musical contemplation the soul is in silent harmony, no material object solicits its senses, no concept its intelligence. For these three reasons music is the deepest and fullest of the arts, the one in which man finds the most intimate fusion of all the planes of his being that his vertical posture had separated.

Following this path we come to observe that the scale of the arts according to the weight of matter they need to manifest themselves arises out of no mere caprice of the observer. There lurks in human nature a subtle relation between the material and the intellectual—we shall come to it again further on—which may be due to the fact that matter is the thing that can be measured, and the intellect is the faculty that measures things. *Pensare*, to think, to weigh. The more matter in the work of art, the more thought. But there are two ways of carrying thought for the work of art: in the work itself, or in the artist. Or, perhaps more clearly, if the work of art is a state of mind that is transmitted, it may carry its thought in the state of mind or in the mind which enters into that state. The first mode is active and direct; the second, indirect and passive. The first may ruin the work, the second raises its worth.

The first mode is dangerous because by meddling with the state of mind the intellect cools the emotion. There is a case in French poetry, possibly trivial and even comic, yet useful as an illustration precisely because it is an extreme case of the trouble. André Chenier describes with a tender emotion the feelings of a young girl sentenced to death by a revolutionary court. Here are his famous lines:

> *Quand au mouton bêlant la sombre boucherie*
> *Ouvre ses cavernes de mort*
> *Pâtres, chiens et moutons, toute la bergerie*
> *Ne s'informe plus de son sort.*
> *Les enfants qui suivaient ses ébats dans la plaine*
> *Les vierges aux belles couleurs*
> *Qui le choyaient en foule, et sur sa blanche laine*
> *Entrelaçaient rubans et fleurs*
> *Sans plus penser à lui, le mangent . . .*

and here the poet begins to think and collapses into ridicule:

> *. . . s'il est tendre.*

This case is, of course, quoted rather as a caricature of the havoc which the meddling of the intellect may cause in the esthetic emotion. Other cases less extreme abound, especially in France—for instance, in Voltaire's theatre. Nor is English literature free from them either, as the poetry of Wordsworth shows. The most famous case, might well be that of George Bernard Shaw, a spirit of more light than fire, doomed by his ever-meddling intellect to a certain poetical incapacity which deprives his brilliant work of much universality and perennity.

This danger, which consists in placing the 'state of mind' on too high a plane in the vertical scale, threatens equally, if for different reasons, the plastic arts and literature. The plastic arts need the intellect in order to handle concrete objects. The present tendency towards abstraction in painters and sculptors, intellectualistic though it may seem at first, might well be due to a drive to free esthetic emotion from the sway of the intellect, to create pure painting and pure sculpture as poets are endeavouring to write pure poetry and as musicians have for centuries composed pure music. True, the onlooker is at times left with the feeling that 'the remedy has been worse than the disease'. Not a few of the works of abstract art suffer from too much intellectualism.

For poetry the problem is not the same. Poetry is esthetic emotion expressed in words. Words are vessels for concepts. No artist will find it harder than the poet does to make his emotion bear on other things than concepts. Not until the twentieth century have poets achieved this prowess, and even so not always very successfully. Popular Spanish poetry has succeeded in this earlier and more frequently; perhaps because time and oral transmission have gradually ground away the initial logical form. This is for instance the case of that masterpiece, the *Ballad of Count Arnaldos*. But the literary art stretches from pure poetry to all sorts of 'letters' in which the dosage of poetry and of other elements, more or less intellectual, varies from nought to one hundred per cent. Poetry, therefore, the core of the literary art, is ever threatened in literature by this, so to speak, lateral intrusion of intellectualism. Hence 'didactic poetry' (which in fact is neither), *pièces à thèse* and other such horrors.

Perhaps for the same reason, a certain reserve, a certain reluctance even towards perfection, may be observed in not a few artists. Wouldn't perfection be nearly always due to too much intellect? Can perfection ever go without a certain coldness? Sert used to say that from the perfection of Velázquez the next stage could be nothing but colour photography; while from Goya's imperfection flowed a whole century of European painting. Since the purpose is to communicate a state of mind, an emotion, it may well be that perfection cools emotion in the artist himself, and not merely in the beholder. The revolution launched by Picasso in our century might be described as a *pronuncia-*

*miento* against perfection. Insofar as it *rises* against the predominance of the intellect, it is a vertical movement, a rising of the heart against the tyranny of the brain, of the impatience of vertical genius against the patience of the horizontal talent.

So far, the dangers of the intrusion of the intellect on the artist's *state* of mind. But the activity of the intellect may also be at work not in the state of the mind but in the artist's mind itself; and on this we may be about to meet quite a confusion. There are many artists who, as all-round human beings, are spontaneous, primitive, uncouth, even illiterate, yet they are good artists for all that. *But great artists have always been men of an intellect out of the common.* Art is life and not mere intelligence; but intelligence is life also, and if art springs from experience why exclude intellectual experience from the soil wherefrom it springs? The work of art transmits a state of mind. There are, therefore, three elements in it: state, mind, and transmission. Three concurring criteria to judge the work. The first two being equal, the work will be the greater, the greater the mind.

Everything tallies. For what we require is that in the work of art a great intellect is felt to *vibrate*—not that it manifests itself directly at the moment the work is born. Not that the artist conceives on his intellectual level, since art must be born at the level of emotion; but that when he happens to be living at his intellectual level, he lives deeply. We meet again a requirement already defined: that the work of art be born at the level of emotion but *after* the other levels have been gathered together and united in it.

Of the three criteria by which to judge a work of art, the weightiest is the third: what sort of a man is expressing himself in the work? Of course, the two first standards must be assumed to be satisfied to a degree: there must be a good enough artificer, and a good enough artist; or, in other words, the work must manifest talent and emotion. But, in the end, what is measured in terms of admiration, what is impressed into human history, is the *height*, the greatness, the stature of the vertical urge within the work. Benvenuto Cellini, Charles Baudelaire, Oscar Wilde were artificers and artists; but the great human creators rise above them by the sheer stature of their spirit—Leonardo, Beethoven, Shakespeare. In these giants men feel their own manhood exalted to the upper limits of their aspiration.

Arts there are which blend together elements of time and space. They are the plastic arts of movement, and in particular, the theatre (with its modern developments, the film and television), opera, ballet, and bull-running.[1] They all have in common the use of the human body as the chief instrument for their plasticity, though they differ in the way they use it.

The theatre is a literary art in that its core is poetry and its medium the word. As such, it is an art of time. But it is also an art of space in that it presents itself to the onlooker as a series of pictures or as a picture in motion. This plastic movement is ruled and determined by the literary movement of the work, by its inner poetry; and the art of the stage director consists precisely in creating the harmony required between the inner poetry of the work, as imagined by the dramatist, and the plastic, visible poetry with which it will be expressed on the stage. The blending of the two poetries *realizes* the dramatic work, which in the book lies uncreated or rather only potentially created, like the picture no one has seen in the cellar of a gallery.

The theatre may well be the most exacting of the literary arts in point of a vertical component. In the novel, even in pure poetry, it is possible to conceal a certain horizontal trend in the work, due to an excess of intellectual control. The artist, for lack of genius, may have failed to gather together with enough vertical vigour all the levels of his being that must or should ripen before expressing them-

[1] 'Bullfighting' is an inaccurate and inadequate name.

selves in his work; and yet he may succeed in simulating a work of full humanity—thanks to a talent which will enable him to replace the emotion he is not feeling with the reflection of intellectual light. This shortcoming, which the book may at times screen out of sight, will soon come out on the stage. If the work is lacking in genius, in vertical vigour strong enough to bring action out at all the vital levels of the characters, it will fall as a mere intellectual scheme of life that few spectators will be able to accept as life itself.

Technical progress has allowed the development of that kind of tinned theatre known as the film, but the very conditions in which it is produced tend to turn it into a different sort of art. Or at least they should. Too many films deserve that name—tinned theatre; though the better producers do realize the possibilities of the new art and the wide avenues it opens for imagination and even fantasy. Traditionally the theatre remains too much attached to realism, too closely limited by its conscious or subconscious fidelity to an objective representation of events. None but the greatest artists have succeeded in evading themselves from the prison of a realistic stage. The trouble may come from the strictly three-dimensional stage–space. The technique of photography offers its marvellous possibilities to the film producer, for it enables him to escape from the three-dimensional space through the fourth dimension of fantasy and dreams. Thus it would be precisely through motion–photography that the theatre could escape from its 'photographism'. The usual struggle will soon appear. The artist who tries such a liberation will need all his vertical vigour to conquer the inertia of the realistic cows.

If the theatre depends for its working on two artists, author and stage director, the opera depends on three, its authors being two, the poet and the composer. Seldom, therefore, does this art reach so close a unity as it did in the case of Wagner, who was his own poet. There may be cases when the split between the two authors becomes only too apparent, as in the case of Mozart, an incomparable genius and talent, at times at loggerheads with a scribbler of easy shallow talent and no genius—the outcome being a hybrid work in which the vertical strains of the musician spring in full splendour through the incurably horizontal, humdrum movement of the libretto.

Opera is a standing insult to common sense. Urgent affairs are interminably sung and repeated; secrets are vociferated; dying persons who should be breathless pour forth torrents of voice; everything seems to induce the audience to believe that they have been allowed to witness the goings on in a lunatic asylum. And yet opera as an art flourishes ever. Why? Because the spectator feels and enjoys the unsurpassed gift with which music has been endowed by nature, no other than that of providing a direct immediate expression for human emotions. It is this gift of music, that it utters human emotion, which enables the audience to enjoy the work of art even when it neither hears nor understands what is being sung. The music is sufficient. The spectator would no doubt enjoy it better were he able to follow the literary text as well, but the musical text is often all he needs for his good evening. Thus can we understand the success of *Don Giovanni*. We need not bother about Da Ponte.

In turn, its literary weight lends substance to the opera which, otherwise, might lose itself in nebulous forms of a vague philosophy or neat embroidery of melodic filigree. One marvels at the way in which the psychological insight Mozart reveals in such works as *Figaro* and *Don Giovanni* seeps through to his contemporary symphonies, endowing them with a human depth they might have missed without the inspiration of the operas, still living in the composer's mind. Only Mozart in person could reveal how much of *Don Giovanni* echoes in the Prague Symphony. As, on the other hand, music is the art in which it is easiest to offset mere intellectualism, for music is pure emotion, operas, unless they are too bad, do usually succeed in gathering together into one single emotion the whole usually separate levels of human life.

The ballet is a kind of opera in which the literary expression is entrusted to a rhythmic set of gestures. Bolívar used to say that dancing was the poetry of movement. The ballet amounts to a plastic art in which movement is included as yet another dimension, thereby achieving a synthesis of music, painting, and sculpture. If we conceive pantomime as a dramatic art without words, ballet might be seen as a mimic opera in which the dancers are supposed to interpret the action of the play.

This art allows of many styles, according to the taste of the author and of his interpreters. We begin to sense the growing importance of the executant. Obviously, the arts of the stage differ from the rest by virtue of the special importance of the performer, whose own body becomes an instrument of the work of art. This personal service to the art by the artist–actor, singer, dancer, or *torero*, is already at work in music—orchestras, soloists, singers—whose interpretations must, for good or ill, collaborate with the author's conception in the actual, final work as it is lived. Something similar was noted in the case of the inevitable collaboration between the author and the stage director or producer. In ballet, it is far more important because the dancing body is a far more direct *instrument* of the art; and as the human body could not possibly enter into any artistic activity without engaging all its ultrabodily faculties, it is safe to say that the ballet will be the fuller the more vertical it is.

There are two forms of dancing, both vertical: the French and the Spanish. (I do not deny, rather do I appreciate the others, though I do not deal with them here.) More art than nature the first, more nature than art the second. Or—to return to a former theme—more talent than genius the French, more genius than talent the Spanish.

The opera dancer, French style, is an abstract stylization of femininity (style, form, talent). A woman streamlined to look and move like a top, a geometric figure, a dancing intellect, she controls her movement with her brain, where resides the command centre of the whole dance. The current of vital energy falls from the brain to the limbs and runs to flow towards the earth like an electric fluid escaping through the toe. By contrast, in the Spanish *bailaora* the vital energy seems to surge up from the earth to penetrate the whole body of a natural woman and, having set alive all and every one of her forms with the same powerful rhythm, to burst forth, an invisible flame upwards beyond her head. This is the quality—a supreme dynamic verticality, a power of human synthesis—that endows Spanish dancing with its world-wide appeal.

Following this line of thought we may hope for a better understanding of what Anglo-Saxons describe most inaccurately as 'bullfighting'. *Toreo* is a space–time, plastic–musical art, akin to the ballet though differing from it in a number of important aspects. To begin with, it is a 'lived' art, or a synthesis of art and life, since what is being 'shown' is actually happening. The daggers are not wooden, the shots are not blank. The bull dies and at times the *torero* also. This is a fundamental difference.

It may be a cause of the widespread errors on the subject of *toreo* that are so prevalent among persons endowed with more kindness than critical judgment; the other chief cause of these errors being to consider it as a game or sport rather than as an art. When they realize that what is shown does actually happen, while most art is often just make-believe, most people find it hard to accept *toreo* as an art at all. A Titian nude is not a woman; it is just a set of colours laid on a canvas to make you almost believe there is a woman there. So where there is no make-believe there is no art.

This, however, is but a hasty conclusion. There is such a thing as the art of making you believe, and the art of convincing. There is even the art of conquering. *Toreo* is an art, and a *torero* who is not an artist is not a *torero*. For the painter, the matter to be mastered is colour; for the poet, words; for the musician, sounds. For the *torero*, the matter to be mastered is danger. To be brave is not enough for a *torero*, just as wielding a palette and brush is not enough to be a painter. The artist must prove himself capable of transmitting an emotion of beauty; the *torero* does it by imparting form and movement, i.e. sculpture and music, to the group bull—man. *Toreo* confronts the vertical man and the horizontal bull in a living rhythm beating on the edge of death—the ever renewed drama of the motionless moving tree and the 'fierce' cow, in which the moving tree kills the cow, towering above her by all the height of his intelligence, will, and artistic sensibility.

I trust I am not mistaken in surmising that Leonardo had been meditating on such things when he created one of his finest masterpieces, the *St. Anne*, to be seen in the Musée de Louvre.[1] Other pictures have I seen that generate a keener pleasure—those luscious Titians of Madrid, those rich Tintorettos of Venice; or that irradiate a more fiery passion, such as the flame-like shapes in El Greco; or that stand more serene in their beauty, such as the canvasses of Raphael; or that suggest unimaginable depths of human experience, sucn as Rembrandt's rabbis; or that seem happily to fuse time and eternity, as does Velázquez so simply; or that revel in an orgy of human turbulence, such as the violent scenes of Goya. But I always come back to this almost miraculous *St. Anne*. By no means a perfect picture. Experts are of opinion that only the landscape, the figure of St. Anne, and the right arm of the Virgin are by Leonardo. The composition is also his, and it is certainly not one of his best: for the body of the Virgin sitting on her

[1] The rest of Chapter 5 is adapted from a lecture delivered at the American Academy of Arts & Letters in 1957.

mother's knees is far too high for our pleasure, and it seems that this defect might have been avoided.

Physically, therefore, the composition is not good. But on a higher plane, what a magnificent message! The scene is conceived as a cascade falling from left to right; from St. Anne's face to her daughter's head; from the Virgin to her son; from the Infant Jesus to the lamb. And the attitudes are all significant.

The lamb is looking upwards, not precisely at the Child but at the two women above; the Child has his arms busy with the lamb, and his head turned towards his Mother; the Virgin has her arms and eyes on her Child; St. Anne keeps her arms visibly away from all action and looks definitely down on the back of her daughter's head, with a smile indrawn which is one of Leonardo's triumphs as a painter of the spirit.

For St. Anne's smiling eyes look at the Virgin's head and yet look inwards. It is a smile, it is indeed a face, that Leonardo will often paint in other contexts and moods: notably in his *St. John the Baptist* and in his *Bacchus*. For him it must have meant the highest and most ineffable of the mysteries, the source of all life, the Spirit.

This conclusion is strengthened by a scrutiny of the study in charcoal on brown paper in Burlington House, London— a composition far less evolved, in which St. Anne, on the same (physical) level as the Virgin, looks at her and points to Heaven with the same gesture he was to give to St. John, and also to Bacchus, and to St. Thomas in *The Last Supper*. The Burlington House study is a key to Leonardo's intention when painting his *St. Anne*.

The cascade evidently meant to symbolize the spiritual, the conscious, the child-like and the animal phases or planes in man's life and when the picture is thus interpreted, it becomes far more significant than the happy family photograph it seems to be at first.

Art is power over matter directed to achieve an end. Fine arts are forms of such power when the aim in view is beauty. Beauty is spiritual irradiation. A work of art must therefore convey the spirit, or if you prefer it so, life. We admire a work of art when it conveys life.

We do not, however, believe in 'slices of life'—a phrase one often heard half a century ago, and which can be read at times even nowadays. We believe that there are no such things as 'slices of life', because once you slice life all you get is meat. So, since a work of art cannot aim at conveying all life, life in its entirety, it must limit itself to a part of it. And, if it is a true work of art, this part will be so conceived as to be alive, that is, organically connected with the rest, and to partake of that privilege of all living things: that they sum up and reflect within their limited scope the whole of life. Blake put it, forever:

> To hold infinity in the palm of your hand
> And eternity in an hour.

A work of art, therefore, can be judged according to the 'art' in it or to the 'work' in it, i.e. according to the power over matter that it reveals or the aim this power is made to serve. And this aim itself, being the rendering of a moment of life, will offer itself to our criticism under a twofold aspect: that of the quality of the moment, and that of the quality of the life. Ultimately, it is the quality of the artist's life that is at stake.

Is it then too fanciful to imagine that art may live in any of the four planes symbolized in Leonardo's *St. Anne*? Or possibly, that expressing, as it always does, the nature of man on these four planes, it may stress any one of the four more than the rest? Am I too rash in thinking for instance that, in several ways, Zola, Goya, and Picasso often remain on the lamb's plane? Please note that I am not reflecting on the power of these artists. Power has nothing to do with it. You may whisper Beethoven's Ninth Symphony and bellow the latest jazz cacophony, or vice versa, without touching on their respective meanings; I am only referring to the level of life that they express. Zola, Goya, and Picasso are artists of magnificent power. But what do they express? On what level do they live? Or rather at what level do they exist? My suggestion is that often—by no means always but often—their level is that of Leonardo's lamb.

Then comes the Child. He looks at his mother but his arms are round the Lamb. His action draws him to the animal. His mind half guesses already where he belongs. Could we not place here the bulk of the artistic production of modern times that seeks a wide appeal? All art—plastic, musical or literary—usually described as 'realistic'; the art, for instance, dear to the nineteenth-century bourgeois or the twentieth-century politburo leader, Monsieur Homais and Mr. Shepilov. At its lowest level, the mass of successful, photographic novels; chromo-lithographs; at its highest level, Bouguereau, possibly even Meissonier. It is an art that that must have a story. Note the child's arms, busy in the animal world, the world of action. And this is the moment to remember those good souls who now and then try to represent *Hamlet* so as 'to concentrate on the story', as they say.

We are here in the childish stage of art. It must be simple. It must be straightforward. It must not conceal second or third meanings. It must tell its story simply and just as it is. It must, nevertheless, leave a kind of feeling that it might mean more if it only dared, but just dares not.

But there is another and a deeper art that also belongs to the childish phase or plane. It is that actually created by gifted children, or in many of the masterpieces found in prehistoric caves, or among savage tribes; expressions of man not precisely in the subconscious but in the unself-conscious state, in which freedom from intellectual fetters

120

leads to a delightful freshness. They remain predominantly poems of action—the Child's arms round the lamb—but the lack of self-criticism that led to sophistication and disastrous results in the first case, allows an innocence to blossom that saves the work.

Whence the difference? Perhaps in that this second and deeper kind of childish art is genuine and natural, since it manifests itself in circumstances comparable to actual childhood; while that mediocre, realistic art which strikes us as childish is perhaps more related to a kind of backwardness. Nor could we leave out of account here, if only by a kind of association, that quite a number of sideshows and would-be successes in the art of our day may be due to the conscious use of childish ways and styles once genuine in their childishness, but which once imitated become infantile.

So much for the Child.

There is, however, a continuity, no actual break, between this stage and the next. The Virgin is looking at her child, and her arms are also busy with him. In the previous stage, the Child's action was on the Lamb; his thought, the very little there was, was on the Virgin. Now, both thought and action are on the Child—that is, on Life. We have attained a fully grown stage. Art conscious of itself. All works, however fine, could come under this category, since we are here in the realm where the mind meets life.

But there sits above it all that haunting smile, those eyes looking at the same time at the whole outward and at the whole inward scene, at nature and at the poet himself. And this is the highest plane an artist can attain. It may be admitted that something of this plane must descend like manna on the next plane below for a work of art to be truly great. But above even the greatest stand a few that seem to have been naturally born at this height—the Spiritual Song of St. John of the Cross, the C minor quartet of Beethoven, *Anthony and Cleopatra* by William Shakespeare, *The Brothers Karamasov* by Dostoyevsky, this *St. Anne* of Leonardo . . .

Are these observations altogether idle? Are we not nowadays traversing a perilous era in our artistic evolution, owing to our neglect of what we have to say and our obsession with the ways of saying it? One might be tempted to apply to much modern art a cruel dictum: that it says forcibly what might have been left unsaid. All art moves on two poles: the object and the artist. We like to call classic that art which gravitates rather towards the object; romantic, that which gravitates towards the artist. If we accept these terms, we may well consider that art has never been more romantic than today, for never in the history of art has the object been more ruthlessly sacrificed to the whims and even to the brutalities of the artist. Indeed, in some cases, the dream of our contemporaries would be to create without an object at all—as in abstract painting or abstract music.

Must we then go back to the quaint old belief that art consists in imitating nature? Far from it. Colour photography does it much better. But the relations between art and nature are subtle. No imitation; but no divorce either.

One might be tempted to define the arts as: *variations on the theme of life*. What else is a novel, or a play? The definition suits even abstract art, for an abstraction is a variation on the theme of life consisting in cutting out a certain number of notes from the melody of nature.

This way of seeing art has the advantage of keeping art and nature together, while emancipating art from that servility to nature which was implied in 'imitation'. No. Art does not imitate nature; yet it does need nature in order to wander away from it, to set going variations from it.

We must recognize in art a nature that was—a nature that was the pretext, the starting point, the theme on which we are writing our variations. But if all we can do is to repeat the theme, we do not deserve the name of artists. We are only exponents, or interpreters.

Now life is full of themes. And there will be a first selection of the artists according to the life themes they are apt to choose for their variations. They may go for them to any of the three lower planes of Leonardo's *St. Anne*: the animal, the childish, the human. In rare moments of grace, they may reach the level of St. Anne herself.

Was ever any truly great work of art conceived without at least an inkling of inspiration from this highest level? But then, there are also combinations of the four levels, which correspond to natural affinities; and, in particular, intellectual–animal and spiritual–childish combinations. Mozart is often spiritual–childish (St. Anne–Infant Jesus); Beethoven is nearly always intellectual–animal (Virgin Mary–Lamb); until towards the end of his life, in his last quartets, he reaches the St. Anne level with a degree of deliberate consciousness that may be symbolized as St. Anne–Virgin, i.e. a combination rarely found in Mozart.

We are nowadays in an era that unflinchingly, if at times morbidly, looks downward from levels that hardly bear such an attitude. Hence the child–animal combination of much of our modern literature and plastic art. Perhaps it is no more than a descent into Hell seeking a further ascent on solider ground than—we fancy—our ancestors stood on or endeavoured to climb. But it certainly limits our art at best to the intellectual–child–animal combinations of Stravinsky, Picasso, and Brecht.

In a sense, all this corresponds to the profound disintegration of the classic architecture of our psyche under the joint attack of the three great Jewish prophets who missed the bus of the Bible: Marx, Freud, and Einstein. But the idea that artists must perforce represent their age may be overdone. This idea is more convincing as applied to the bulk of the artists than to the truly great ones. Indeed one might venture the suggestion that an artist is great insofar as he transcends his age and reaches that level of the human which is common to all ages. Bach is greater in his great

*Toccata and Fugue* than on his usual, albeit excellent level, where he is merely of his time. Mozart, in tune with his time in *Figaro* and *Eine kleine Nachtmusik*, is above it in his Prelude for Strings, in his last symphonies, and in much of his *Don Giovanni*. Beethoven does utter his time in his Fifth and Sixth symphonies, perhaps even in the Ninth, but rises far above it in his last Quartets. Cervantes expresses his day in the *Novelas Ejemplares* but the timeless–universal in his *Don Quixot*. And El Greco is always above time.

We are fortunate today in possessing artists of great power. But we do not seem, as an era, epoch, or generation, to be so fortunate with regard to high-level artists, owing perhaps to the downward trend of our day; the dispersive and even destructive character of much of what we do and are, the strains and tensions of a mankind in travail. Hence, despite much admirable work, the generally unsatisfactory character of the art of our age and its lack both of unity and of truly outstanding men, endowed with spiritual power.

For in the end the highest aim of a work of art is to convey the spirit; to be a butterfly of time on wings of eternity.

# 6

It was at this point that Poppy entered the stage. Her old-gold coat shining with a recent brushing, her pointed, inquisitive nose, her large velvety eyes, everything in her alive with curiosity and appetite, she came straight towards the table on which, among the papers, she had spotted the silver basket full of her favourite sugar-coated pine seeds. Sundry gestures intended as hints, by themselves or in adequate combination—lip-licking, alternative glances at the silver basket and at its owner—having yielded no results, she resolved to have recourse to more drastic measures, and she 'treed' herself on her hind legs in the, for a dog, official mendicant position.

Odd, isn't it?, that dogs should rise on their hind legs in order to beg. A posture, by the way, which does not suit them. Nature has denied them the rotating motion of the forearm and so they are not able to turn the hollow hand upwards, in the shape of a begging bowl; and there they stand, with their poor hands hanging useless from their wrists. No. Dogs are no good as beggars. Beggary is only fit for human beings.

At this stage in my lucubrations, I was seized by a startling thought. I had so often wondered whence and from whom that impulse might have come which had driven the quadruped to rise on his hind legs. But could it be *this*? Could it be some urge similar to that which induces dogs to 'tree' themselves so as to beg for a sugar-coated pine seed? Begging, then, is the word. But for what? And from whom? From whom, it is pretty obvious. Who could it be but the Creator? He alone stands in creation as high at least above man as man stands above animals. If ever a four-footed beast dreamt of immortality, he might have thought of begging for it as dogs do for sugar. Trees must have seemed to that ambitious animal so close to heaven, with their arms high towards the blue. Who knows? Perhaps by dint of raising our forepaws, now free from the height of the body which had nailed them to the ground . . .

Fancies. Variations on the theme of Poppy and the sugar-coated pine seeds. But the fact is that immortality is the pine-seed silver basket of all human dogs 'treed' up like beggars before the deity. 'Oh Lord,' they seem to implore, 'grant us a few centuries longer of this dog of a life You have dealt out to us with so niggardly a hand.' And on this theme there is also the possibility of adopting a vertical or a horizontal attitude.

The problem might even be schematized *more geometrically*. If we figure a human being by a point at which two straight lines meet, representing his paternal and his maternal lines and each formed by a succession of such individual points, it will be possible for us to imagine present, past, and future mankind as a plane formed by all these individual points and woven by all those family lines; and it will be easy for us to visualize this plane as horizontal since it spreads along the line of time, which, flowing as it does like a river, does suggest a horizontal line, if slightly sloping.

That being so, the problems of forelife and afterlife would then amount to that of the existence or inexistence of an individual factor independent of both paternal and maternal constituents. For geometrical purposes, this factor might be conceived as a vertical line perpendicular to the plane of mankind. Thus defined, the problem amounts to wondering whether we should understand a human being as wholly determined by his paternal and maternal genes plus the outcome of their interaction, or as including also in his constitution an element coming from or through neither of his ancestors.

Does biology answer this question in a confident and convincing way? I do not know. I surmise that horizontal biologists—how–scientists—will refuse to admit the existence of life–factors other than those that come from and through the two progenitors; while vertical biologists—what– or why–scientists—will keep their views to themselves and wait. Still, those who would deny would certainly not lack facts and data to prop up their scepticism. As here outlined, the problem does not seem to encourage any belief in pre- or post-life. A *future* has no sense outside a belief in transmigration. A future life without a past life does not seem very convincing. Why should the future *begin* here and now? Since the future is just a past which the present has not yet swallowed, it is hard for human reason to conceive a future life unless there is a past life also. And for a belief in a past life we lack the necessary foundations.

There are conjectures. The immense knowledge evinced by some child prodigies—Pascal, Mozart—and even the astonishing speed of intellectual progress in all infants, are pointers to a previous life. In general, all the *vertical* upsurges of creative power we have here described as 'genius' suggest some sort of pre-existence—and yet, we feel, it hardly goes beyond a mere suggestion. And a similar observation would be valid for certain reminiscences of times and places one finds now and then at the far end of one's memory, with no particular foundation in present life experience.

The continuity of ancestral features, both physical and psychical, on the horizontal plane, is beyond question. The point need not be laboured, since this aspect of things is not being debated. Yet, it must be owned that such an undoubted continuity of features along the horizontal plane of succession does strengthen the stand of those who deny the existence of a vertical component in the newborn being. It happens that a newborn baby is the very image of his paternal grandfather only to appear within three months as the very image of a maternal aunt, whereupon his features will begin freely to wander along the two diverging ancestral spaces open to it. It happens that a person is like his father in his body and like his mother in point of character. All this mobility of the human person, this free access he seems to enjoy to his vital past, does suggest—though not altogether prove—a full genetic determination, and therefore the inexistence of a vertical component.

When an outstanding genius appears in a family, so to speak, without warning, our doubts are revived. In some cases a materialistic explanation might be plausibly based on heredity. Thus, Mozart, Beethoven, might be cases of an abnormally favourable growth of genes that had already given forth musically gifted progenitors; though even this could hardly establish the exceptionally creative power of these two composers, for whom their inherited musical gift was no more than an instrument. But there are other cases—Leonardo, Pascal, Shakespeare, Goya—in which no explanation seems possible other than the unexpected irruption of a vertical component almost volcanic in its power; which, once admitted, would also provide a better hypothesis for the Mozart–Beethoven cases. It cannot be denied, though, that even in the case of the unexpected genius of the Leonardo series, a better knowledge of genetics might provide an explanation independent of any vertical component.

Nor is this all that can be said against the existence of a vertical component, or in other words, against survival. There are further obstacles raised, curiously enough, not merely by the corporeal but also by the extra-corporeal aspect of the human person. As for the first aspect, everybody knows that the body is indispensable for life—at any rate as we know it. No one has ever seen or heard an extra-corporeal life. The cases quoted from hagiographies or from the experiences of spiritualists may convince some but can hardly be adduced as proofs endowed with a universal validity. Man's life may or may not be identical with that of his body; but it is only through the life of his body that it becomes manifest. When his body dies, man dies.

True, the body is an illusion, not unlike that other illusion —a river. The waters of a valley will flow along a certain bed; and we describe as *a river* (ever the same) those waters (never the same) whose ephemeral present is now assuming the peculiar form the valley determines for them. The body is a valley that shapes the flow of food passing through it, and which, in the ephemeral hour in which we behold it, thus takes on the familiar shape. Our body is therefore the form that our being imprints on the matters that feed it.

This being, however, had to be created through the sexual union of two bodies. The continuity of bodily life is a fact. We know no life but the corporeal, or at any rate, none but that which manifests itself in and through the body. We are not for an instant stepping out of the horizontal plane of physical bodies. Even if we took for granted the existence of that vertical component—an axis for past and future lives—it would have to incarnate in the horizontal plane of physical bodies in order to live here and now.

Our personal experience does, now and then, also suggest a material explanation for life. The *idée fixe*, for instance. It happens that the mind, seized by a deep worry or an acute grief, far from shunning it, seems unable to keep itself from falling and falling again into the thought or mood that tortures it. It all happens as if the grief or worry had hollowed out a groove in the brain, into which the meditating mind cannot help dropping like a wheel into the track.

The working of what is known as 'association of ideas' suggests similar images. There are persons who think mostly in chains of related ideas, as if all of the ideas were 'filed' in the brain in physically parallel rows, or tied together by memory with the same link that united them when they 'happened'; so that not merely ideas but even memories, incoherent in themselves but tied together by life—a person and a perfume, a melody and a moment lived under its sonorous shadow—sleep together in the arcana of the sub-conscious; and when one awakes, it awakens the other. This experience, frequent as it is in the psychic life of men, would favour an explanation of the life of the mind by means of physical images such as impressions left on the brain cells.

Finally, there remains another observation of the life of thought: the fact that it develops less by logical steps than in a blind vital evolution. Our way of understanding complex things does not evoke an instantaneous operation, such as the locking of a syllogism-machine, which would occur at the close of a series of clear moves; but on the contrary, a slow and obscure, partly subconscious elaboration, not unlike a fermentation. Rather than of a mathematical demonstration, the understanding of a complex thing would make one think of the way cheese is evolved out of milk through cream accumulated in repose. And this fact, which at first sight would seem to favour a vitalistic rather than a mechanistic view of life, nevertheless favours a deterministic and physico-chemical interpretation, since it suggests that thought is a chemical operation or reaction which needs time.

Here another obstacle bars our way to the acceptance of that vertical component. If we admit it for man, why not also for animals? Intuition refuses to recognize any un-surmountable barrier between man and the 'higher' animals. Hinduism professes transmigration for men and animals; and no observer of men will have failed to note men who are like horses, oxen, swine, or sharks; old women who are in fact cockatoos and many more impersonations (if that is the word) that the popular motherwit is not slow in picking up and expressing in every language. If we are to admit a future life for the grouse shooter, why not also admit it for his dog, and if for the old maid, why not for her cat?

Why not indeed? Someone in us asks the question and

finds no answers, at any rate none to our satisfaction. Yet, at bottom, we feel a doubt. Is it worth while? Are we worthy of it? Is this tragicomedy worth a second evening? The street-corner cobbler who beats his wife every night, the disintegrated marquis who dissolves his rents in whisky, the gangster and the pimp, do they deserve to live after death? And if not, who chooses? And why shouldn't they wonder whether I deserve to survive? I heard once, in Bombay, Auden say—and how could I forget it?—'Of course we know that we are here to help the others, but the trouble is we don't know what the others are here for'. One thing is to love one's neighbour; another one to be able to bear him!

And so we are quietly led to the other row of obstacles against our belief in survival—those coming from extra-bodily considerations. Human life is not contained in the receptacle or skin in which nature packed its organs. The nine gates we read about in a number of Eastern scriptures are open to a traffic between the world within and the world without the skin. The physical being is up to a point contained within the skin full of life which seems to constitute it; but it is plain that if it did not live beyond its bodily limits, just as the psychic being does, its life would be at an end. Every human person, therefore, *lives out of his body as much as contained within it;* and this indisputable observation sheds a penetrating light on the problem of life after death.

The human being is not something mysterious and ethereal squatting in the body as a lodger, in such a way that if his abode crumbles to pieces he can just gather his belongings and move on. This attitude, which is more or less that of spiritualism, may well be somewhat oversimplified. The human being is in the manner of a centre of energy around which a field of forces will develop; and this field of forces is not unlike that which nowadways defines an electric, magnetic, or gravitational centre of energy; though the personal centre and its field are far richer and far more complex. The life of a human group—a family, a city, a nation—can be compared with that of a solar system or a galaxy of solar systems composed of suns, planets, satellites, comets and meteors—human beings all, every one of them surrounded by a field of psychic forces emanating from his core.

When death snuffs out one of them, the field of psychic forces that emanated from him while he lived does not go out of action at once. It lasts on, longer in some cases than in others. With the great, the trivial psychical forces which emanated from them die soon, but the more powerful ones remain. The psychic forces that ruled Mozart's relations with the Archbishop of Salzburg, or Beethoven's relations with his nephew, formidable in their respective lives, have vanished; but those emanated from them, which they embodied in their works, live forevermore. In these conditions, what are we to understand as 'survival'? That of the being within the skin? Then only part of the being would in fact survive. That of the being outside his skin? But the human being is so closely intertwined with the beings of others, most of whom remain behind when he dies, that it is hard to imagine how the one who goes can go on living without those parts of him which he has left living in the others.

This dispersion of the being *extramuros* is further complicated by a diversity of the being *intramuros* of which every thoughtful person is aware. At times, attitudes and even deeds of our own surprise us. 'I had no idea I was capable of doing this . . .' 'I did not know I knew that . . .' Man does not know well even his own self. Before such a success, failure, before such good, bad, fine, or unworthy action, issued from his own depths, he will remain dumbfounded, wondering what paternal greatgrandfather or maternal uncle has pushed his elbow, sustained his courage, sharpened his desire, left him in the lurch. Of all this inner crowd, of his little kingdom which (as Shelley said) now and then goes through an insurrection, what is it that survives? And

132

so that vertical line, which we saw rising from the past towards the plane of mankind and beyond to reach upwards towards another mankind in a future life, what would it be carrying above this life but a small part of our self? Religions have, of course, tumbled to this difficulty, and have tried to meet it by denying 'the world' (i.e. our own dispersion into the sea of the others). Christianity warns us against the world, in which it sees one of the three enemies of the soul. Another enemy is the flesh (i.e. the body). In this way does the Christian church prepare the vertical rise of man towards a worldless Heaven, unimaginable for ordinary mortals. Other confessions present the world as an illusion. But who will ever separate in us that which is world from that which isn't?

Reason, then, seems to lead us ever to negative conclusions. *Eppur si muove*. Mankind *wants* another life. I forget who it was who said that since we know this one, which, though real, is so unlikely, why not another one? And man, eager to live on, seizes hold of this argument 'for dear life'. It arms him with strength to struggle against the argument we had just left on top of the field. Precisely because our being pours itself out into the world, it can draw itself in again to pour itself out in another one. True, life is not made up merely of friends, adversaries, and a mass of indifferent ones. It is a vast whole comprising also animals, plants, stars . . . The human being is not merely a centre of emanation of physical forces; he is also a unit of life in this vast whole, which comprises the animals that provide him with meat and milk and eggs, the plants that supply him with vegetables and fruit and feed 'his' animals, the sun that keeps the whole together, the orbits that establish the seasons—in one word the whole world in a solidarity of existence with him. Man as a body, therefore, is a unit of universal life in an earthly context. Does this picture not suggest a kind of incarnation, a descent to conditions and circumstances that reason itself would accept as exceptional?

In order to maintain this proposition one must prove that man is bigger than life. Here Pascal comes to our rescue. *L'homme n'est qu'un roseau, le plus faible de la nature, mais il est un roseau pensant*—words that may not define but do illustrate the situation. By his thought, man is bigger than life; it is hard, therefore, to see how he could be a *mere* product of it. Nor is this a matter of mere thought. The very eagerness with which he asks for more of it, even if it be different, suggests in him a certain independence of *this* life, which feeds, supports, and jails him. And again there lives in him a natural, original, and 'own' energy which recalls Spinoza: *In suo esse perseverare conatur.*

This energy, this perseverance—our intuition feels certain that it does not belong to the physico–chemical or mechanical, not even to the spatial–temporal order. True, when starving or exhausted man may feel his forces sink in proportion to the loss of solar energy on which he depends for his bodily life. But it often happens that physically weak men evince more—well, more *spirit* than the strong and well-nourished ones. Intuition perceives here two kinds of energy, differing in substance and in origin, one physical and the other non-physical. It is not a mere instinct of conservation, which might well be a physico–chemical outcome of that persevering, original energy; it is a source of life power deeper than both the body and the soul that might be identified with the initial impulse received by the Creator.

Before advancing further along this path we had better honestly and openly face the undeniable fact of our time: we are living in an atheistic era. Atheism is in our day the only official and orthodox attitude admissible in the intellectual and academic worlds. He who would now speak in earnest about the Creator will have to be prepared to face an ostracism similar to that which in other centuries punished heresy.

It might be maintained that our atheistic orthodoxy is a result of the predominance of two of man's levels: the rational and the material. We have already met the undoubted affinity that exists between these two levels. The physical world is one that lends itself best—perhaps the only one that lends itself—to being measured; therefore the most rational—or at least so it seemed to be. Now it is true, after the breaking up of the atom, perspectives grow darker and the readiness of things to let themselves be measured grows more and more problematic. This fact, however, does not seem to have impaired as yet the affinity between the rational and the material levels of man.

This combination is particularly vigorous in three of the most intelligent people of the earth: the French, the British, and the Jews. If with different shadings, they are rationalists and determinists; the Frenchman stressing rationalism and general ideas, a network into which he ever hopes to make matter and even life fit; the Englishman stressing matter and observation ('browsing'), on which he builds his empiricism; the Jew with his cold indifference to anything but 'facts', which his hazardous life has bred in him.

Now, the intellectual eminence of these three peoples is not in question. From the sixteenth century on, Europe's cultural life has been led from Paris and London; and from the nineteenth, in which the emancipation of the Jewish people begins in earnest, the Jews have contributed to human culture a harvest of creative minds incomparably higher (in proportion to their numbers) than that of any other people on earth. Modern cultural life receives its major impulse, its main tone, its atmosphere, mostly from these three highly deserving peoples. And all three, by the very inner shape of their spirit, are prone to atheism.

It must be owned that the chief responsibility for present-day atheism must be attributed to the several confessions,

135

religions, or churches. Religions may be likened to confessional nations. They suffer from all the shortcomings and excesses of nationalism. It would be less than seemly for a national of the country that knew the most sinister Inquisition in human history to point his finger at any one nation in this respect; but he might be allowed to state that next to racial nationalism, confessional nationalism has proved one of the most sanguinary and cruel of the human passions. When the man of science, sick at heart, turns his back on all that, locks himself in his laboratory and will not hear a word about God, who would reproach him for it?

Religions are, moreover, a breeding ground for repulsive superstitions, which some of them reject with one hand and bless with the other. From Europe we look down our noses at the Kashmiris, who are capable of killing and being killed for the sake of a hair of Mohammed's beard; but no Asian would find it hard to look down on the shameless trade in ex-votos and relics that flourishes in certain religious zones of the West. Nor even if we brushed aside all these humble miseries would the critic lack other confessional errors to report in the fields of mythology, archaeology, and indeed history, which do but increase atheism as a reaction of intelligent people whose taste is being offended.

Atheism is then the mode, or perhaps the style, of our era. But it is also something deeper. It is the only form of cosmogony that fits the Franco–Anglo–Jewish rationalistic determinism, and which in its turn expresses a need of the modern spirit. This fact emerges to the light of our day in certain aspects of our communal life, such as the predominance of metal and glass in architecture, and the rectangular style these materials dictate. Even before the triumph of glass and metal, architecture had begun to express this, at bottom, horizontal spirit. Take the impressive mass of the Rockefeller Center, bearing in mind and eye the Roman Catholic cathedral close by: though the modern building towers above the cathedral, the cathedral is vertical while the Center is but a pile of horizontal levels. This observation fits in with another that might be offered on the psychology of the American: even though he may be, and often is, more intelligent, kindlier, more generous than the European, *he is shorter by one storey*. (Something similar occurs, by the way, if we compare Shakespeare and Calderón. Far bigger within every one of the levels common to both, Shakespeare is shorter by one storey than the Spaniard.)

This modern spirit, all in metal–force, clarity–glass, and horizontal cubism, acquires strength and universality through the chief event of our time—the scientific explosion. The advance of science which begins in earnest with Galileo and Newton, takes on speed and volume through the eighteenth and nineteenth centuries to reach, in the twentieth, such a degree of fecundity and vigour that it allows us to describe it without undue fancy as an explosion. The discoveries of our day are so many and so varied that they have blurred out of history the figure of the all-round scientist (if such a figure ever existed), forcing the scientist to a higher degree of specialization. Analysis is the dominant mood; the dominant scientist is the horizontal or 'how' type. The analytical era that began in the sixteenth century, to which mankind owes so much, is today at the very apex of its discovering activity. Synthesis is looked upon with suspicion; it sounds like literature. Literature itself becomes analytic for fear of being despised—as literature. Synthesis is not in the *fashion*.[1]

But if we stand back and look at the debate, we soon discover that the respective positions of the atheist and the deist are not symmetrical. The deist and the atheist are not

[1] True, there is a rapid evolution towards a confrontation of sciences in the study of certain phenomena; and even, perhaps, a hankering towards synthesis. It does not seem, however, at any rate *yet*, strong enough to stem the powerful forces leading to specialization; though it is probably preparing the rise of great why–scientists who would warrant our brightest hopes.

like two observers watching the same object from opposite sides, about whom an impartial arbiter could hold a balanced opinion. The man who does not see God and the man who sees God are not contradicting each other, any more than the man for whom music means nothing can be said to contradict Mozart. They are rather like two spectators of the same play, who interpret it in different ways—possibly both far from the author's own intention.

God cannot be proved. He can be guessed, divined (please note this word), adumbrated, 'caught in the act', felt. The atheist is entitled to his negation, since he does not see God; just as a blindman would be entitled to declare black every picture in the British Museum. The point is that the atheist's negation means nothing to the man who has caught a glimpse of God; not only because, since God cannot be proved, He cannot be disproved either, but because the source of knowledge in the one case is not of the same nature as in the other.

No. I am not opposing faith to reason. I am rather contrasting intuition with lack thereof; and when I say *intuition* I realize that the word, rich as it is, is too poor for what I should wish it to suggest. These subjects cannot be handled with a mere cold-blooded logic and a meticulous weighing of words. They need to be received in the mansion of the mind all doors and windows open, at all the levels of the spirit, in one word in a vertical rather than in a horizontal way. For God is the synthesis of all analyses, the vertical of all horizontals, the tree of all cows. And in the pages that follow God will be affirmed and confessed no matter what the French, the British and the Jews may say.

First of all, for things to make sense. Men seem to imagine the Universe in one of only three ways: as the act of a Person, as the consequence of an abstract Principle, or as the working of a Machine. The fashion today favours a combination of the abstract principle and the machine. To reject it does not necessarily mean to accept the first alternative, a Person. Rather should we refuse to fall back on it; for the natural and reasonable attitude would be to think that man is just as unable to imagine God as the mouse or the mosquito is to imagine man. We must, nevertheless, prop our guessing on some concrete image; and, granted this, the image of a Person is the least inadequate of the three, at least as a symbol, if only because we start by acknowledging in the idea of God *an energy, an initiative,* and *an intelligence.*

We have come to this idea from the observation of that 'persevering in his own being' which is the essence of man. Persistence, stubbornness, the will to be and to keep on being one self and not another. This energy is a prime, original fact, and it operates in us before we are aware that it does. It is, therefore, *in* the being before consciousness emerges. It is life before reflection. And no physico–chemical combination could account for it. Original will is at the root of man. It lives in all men. It has the same nature in all. We are, therefore, entitled to think that it manifests the original impulse we received at birth from our Creator.

This initial impulse strikes us intuitively in all creatures. In the dog as in the worm, in the oak as in the grass; and as study teaches us that dog, worm, oak, and grass, though fully autonomous, are all limbs of one single living whole, we are led to see beneath and behind all life the same original impulse received from the Creator.

The will to be is directed by initiative and enlightened by intelligence in a rising degree as we pass from the vegetal to the animal kingdom and, within the latter, from the *lower* to the *higher* animals. The seed once planted, the stem that sprouts will seek to align itself in the prolongation of the radius of the planet, the shortest cut towards light and air, the vertical. What combination of physico–chemical forces regulates this prodigious fact? We do not know. But the tree evinces a most effective combination of (albeit rudimentary) intelligence and initiative.

It is plain that in the observable world, so far, the initiative and intelligence of creatures reach their apex in man. And now we may be beginning to adumbrate the cause of the unity of the human being, whose multiplicity had struck us so much before. If the human being has been compared to a nation in which now and then insurrections and mutinies will break loose, how can there be an insurrection when there is no government? Over and above the multiplicity, there is a unity. And this unity proceeds from the initial impulse received from the Creator, which demands perseverance in one's being.

A strange paradox. For what makes us all be who we are and no other—therefore, all different—is a force emanating from one single Source of energy, the same for all. It is precisely our common divine origin that makes us diversely human. Nor should this seem strange to us if we rely on the only form of creation we know. What is it that makes Lear, Hamlet, Othello, Macbeth, Cleopatra be what they are, so much themselves and so distinct, but the impulse they all receive from the one and only Shakespeare? This is a road we shall have to tread later. For the present all we need do is record that what makes us be what we are is the initial impulse that we received from the Creator—in other words, that in us which comes from God, or else God in us.

And it is here that we might draw the line between animals and man. In animals, the Creator has limited initiative and intelligence to forms and actions that are imitative, *specific* in the sense that they characterize the species; while to man He has granted a share in His creative faculty. This delegation implies initiative to enquire beyond life, and reflection to behold and judge it. When man suddenly discovers that 'somebody in him' has acted in a way he did not expect, so that he stands surprised, who is the effect and who the cause of his surprise? Who is looking at and judging whom? Within the human being there live government and governed, authority and rebellions against it. All this would appear to allow the surmise that the inner authority springs from an origin other than the two ancestries, that the spirit of unity does not flow from the same source as that which leads to dissensions—in other words, that there is, after all, a 'vertical component'.

For the horizontal, ancestral tradition is transmitted to us through our genes—two packs of cards, for all we know, shuffled and cut by Hazard, which deals a few cards to the new-born being for him to play out his life with. The dispensations thus given us seem to come in a rather vague, casual, and haphazard way: the form of the nose and the colour of the eyes mixed up with intellectual speed, courage, gestures, a musical ear, fluency. . . . If unity, government there be, it is not likely to come from such a bric-à-brac of heirlooms; but rather from a drive outside the plane of ancestries, from a vertical impulse.

Which by no means implies—rather the reverse—that such a unifying impulse may not manifest itself also in the body. For the body is not lacking in regions that express the synthesis or wholeness of the being it houses. The hand is one of them. No one who has come across a really competent and gifted hand-reader will allow himself to be dissuaded by rationalistic arguments from the objective value of the lines of the hand. Another synthetic spot is the foot. But the most prodigious and best studied of these whole–revealing places in the body is the iris of the eye, in which every organ of the body is represented with such astonishing exactness that it has proved possible to found on this fact a truly scientific diagnosis. This is yet another of the vertical sciences that horizontal rationalists refuse to accept as such; not without cause, since it implies the victorious irruption of a vertical synthesis on to the field of horizontal analysis.

From this point of vantage our notions of vertical and

horizontal life take on a new significance. We have seen the tree, from its first appearance outside the seed, seeking the vertical, i.e. the prolongation of the line that links it with the centre of the earth. This observation leads to at least two interesting conclusions. *In the world of verticals, there are no parallels.* Cows may stand parallel to each other in their hundreds but no two trees are ever parallel. They diverge directionally, each seeking its own vertical and, though the difference is negligible for two trees close together, it becomes important as the distance grows. These remarks should therefore be added to the passage where we showed that for man to recognize other men by no means implied the existence of a vertical herd.

The second conclusion is that the tree seed, once planted into the earth, *proceeds to get away from the earth by the quickest way leading to heaven.* This grants to the notion of the vertical a new significance. 'High' and 'low', which at first seemed somewhat arbitrary choices due to our having assumed an erect position, now appear in a new light. At whatever spot of the earth we happen to be, 'low' means 'towards the earth and its centre', while 'high' means 'away from the earth'. Heaven does not mean 'on high', it means 'non-earth', an urge towards the spirit, away from incarnation.

We may then interpret the sequence vertical (tree)—horizontal (animal)—vertical (man) as meaning that the way incarnation takes place first, when the tree definitely grows away from the earth, adumbrates man's revolt against it; then life takes on a resigned, accepted form parallel to the surface of the earth, throughout the animal kingdom, and finally rises in revolt again when man stands erect as the tree had done, seeking that vertical which is the shortest way out of the earth.

From all of which can be deduced the vigour of the vertical element in the human being and, therefore, the support that this element lends to the individual will to persevere and to the intuition of an initial divine drive in the innermost man.

Those who, as does Miguel de Unamuno, link the two themes together and make them interdependent, those who value the existence of God as a guarantee of the survival of man, and those who value the stubbornness of the being who perseveres in his own existence as a proof of the existence of God are all entitled to support their respective faiths on the identity that may be established between the will to live and the inner God. Hence that curious utterance: '*My God.*' This 'my God', or God within is no doubt the impulsor who 'treed' the quadruped and incited it to yearn for the tallest possible vertical height.

An act of reciprocity to which reference was made at the beginning of this voyage. Transcendental God made Himself immanent within the being of pre-man to raise him to manhood; and immanent God within man yearns to unite with transcendental God on high. To God immanent within turn the eyes looking inwards of the Buddha, smiling an eternal smile; through the big black eyes of byzantine icons, God immanent within looks at the world; at God transcendent stare the saints in extasis in the Spanish pictures. And to the union of both, passionately yet serenely, aspire the last quartets of Beethoven.

This may well be the core, or one of the cores, of the mystery of the Incarnation. Transcendent God incarnates in men and becomes immanent in them, breaking into tiny bits. And human life consists in an endeavour of all those tiny bits of immanent God to be reunited and reintegrated into the bosom of transcendent God. Hence our vertical yearning.

Were this so, survival would be relieved from that urgency and eagerness which tightens to the breaking point all souls who suffer hunger for eternity. The natural end of the human being would be to sink into the eternity of God, Who is both alpha and omega of his life. Whether he is to reach this ultimate end and supreme destiny at the end of this life or after having lived other lives as well would appear as less weighty. And, it might be argued, the sooner the better.

Eternal life. Future life. The two terms are apt to be interchanged and bandied about as if they were similar. But they convey quite different meanings. Future life is conceived in time, and therefore in space. Eternal life knows neither space nor time. He who yearns for a future life is in fact longing to live on or again the one and only life he knows, this here-and-now earthly life, with its five senses. The fact is often hidden behind rows of convent jam pots, but it is a fact for all that. Hence the revealing contradictions betrayed by many a soul that thinks itself religious; such as thanking God for having saved one's life from shipwreck, fire or illness, i.e. for having adjourned the day of supreme bliss when the religious soul is to behold the face of the Lord.

Eternal life can be conceived only as the return to the bosom of the transcendent God. We must here recall the indigence of this *personal* symbolism and its inadequacy to represent the Creator. Life eternal cannot be merely the return to Father's house, the seeing again of a loved person. It must be something unthinkable and unutterable, of which we only know what it is not. It certainly is not anything that occurs in space and time; and if it means death to the boundaries of the individual it means more life than ever for the spirit which was locked and limited within those boundaries in this life.

In this way not only can eternal (not future) life be seen under a better light but this earthly life also acquires a new sense. It is hard to see what sense this life can have, seen from an atheistic, physico–chemical point of view. If men are mere flesh and bones computers, no apparent reason leaps to the eye for demanding respect for the human person or for granting any value to individual freedom. The present western atheistic era lives in a relative peace as a parasite on the capital of ethics and religion accumulated by Christianity through twenty centuries; but the crimes of Hitler and Stalin should be seen as the sinister heralds of future catastrophes, sure to overwhelm mankind unless the respect for the living God in him is revived in every man.

The historical responsibility of Euramerica at this moment is appalling. Scores of nations have gained or regained their freedom, most of which lack a deeply rooted religious tradition. Now, history and psychology can explain that the European still lives a sufficiently spiritual life as the heir of one of the most vigorous spiritual traditions of mankind; but such explanations would not carry us very far or give rise to much hope in the case of most African and a number of Asian nations. After all, we have seen Hitler emerge within a Catholic environment and Stalin break the wall of a seminary of orthodox priests. The first cases of power-vertigo are observable in Nkrumah's Africa and in Sokarno's Asia. A revision of the basis of belief among Europeans is an urgent task.[1]

Still, these are positive and historical aspects of the problem, and we are not going to invent God so as to spare mankind international disasters. The essence of the problem lies deeper than history or politics. Enough for the present to assert, as has been done, that once the divine principle in man is rejected, the basis for the respect due to the human person vanishes and the foundations of human liberty disappear. Furthermore, why living? Why working? To feed and procreate (or merely fornicate)? Most human beings will not be content with such a dog or cat life. How are we to find a basis for disinterestedness? Who will be able to live in a disinterested way, i.e. above the level of horizontal appetites, if there does not stir in him a vertical longing, the thirst for a reunion of his inner, immanent God and the God transcendent on high?

[1] Since I wrote these lines, events that have occurred in Ghana and in Indonesia have provided a dramatic confirmation of what I wrote.

And here is another marvel: that this tension towards union of the inner God and the God on high is the cause of our activity. What we seek in action is self-knowledge; or, in other words, the fusion and harmony of the inner God Who drives us and the eternal God Who awaits us. Hence our yearning for action at its highest level, that need of truth, goodness, and beauty in action which stands at the core of true 'morals'—a poor, horizontal word, reeking of the herd, and most inadequate to express that inner law which precedes all teachings or influences.

That is why, because it is a live and not merely a written law, the demand for activity and behaviour (i.e. for quantity and quality of action) is creative, since it comes from the Creator. This is a concrete and essential point. Every minute of human life at which a problem arises opens a parting of the ways, a choice. The subject would in vain try to be guided by what he has learnt, or to apply some commandment or norm. He will have to make up *his* mind in his original way—of course, provided he be free. A free man's life is, therefore, a succession of creations, fortunate or otherwise, but new, unique. If he is aware of acting at every moment as a bridge between the inner God Who drives him and the eternal God Who awaits him, his work will live. If not, it will die for evermore.

## 7

So here I am at the end of this voyage, questioning the mystery that is both hidden and revealed by the cow and the tree, this cross or + sign dissociated into components. Horizontal or vertical? Let us remember how we came to meet this disjunctive while beholding nature during one of the stages of our trip. Horizontal or vertical? Concatenation and development of horizontal movements, waves of change such as those in a river, in a herd trotting with a motion parallel to the earth, *or* a series of vertical revelations?

Few minds nowadays seem to trouble about this question. The mere vacillation before the general choice relegates the doubter to intellectual ostracism. Modern biologists know so much that they do not hesitate. Evolution is a fact.[1] Species come from 'older' species and there is nothing more to be said on the 'what'. Only the 'how' has to be elucidated. The horizontal scientist finds in nature the horizontal way of life he himself brings to her.

Yet at times, even in this how–scientist, a vertical outburst awakens wonderings akin to those of a why–scientist. What is it that incites created beings to this constant change? Our image, the river of the waves of change, tacitly assumed that the motive power was the law of gravity, weight, i.e. that the change was a fall; while on the contrary, in life as we observe it on this planet change is a continuous ascent. And here we are not merely dealing with entropy

[1] So I wrote in my Spanish edition and so I translate it. But I must apologize to those biologists who are close enough to my way of thinking. Thus Dr Heinz Dombrowski, in an admirable article, *Das Alter des Lebens*, in the August, 1965 *Bild der Wissenschaft*, D.V.S., Stuttgart.

and the second law of thermodynamics; but with an evolution rising from the amoeba to Leonardo da Vinci—a movement that no biologist, however mechanistic his outlook, will refuse to consider as an ascent.

Everybody knows the official explanation of such an amazing history: nature brings forth many types and the environment gets rid of the least resistant. The 'fittest survive'. Hence, evolution. This explanation, however, explains nothing. To begin with, no one can prove that what survives is the 'fittest'. Then, no one has proved that what is fittest in any one moment and environment is precisely that which leads to the next higher stage in the evolution *upwards*, which has to be explained; and finally, even if we admitted that the rule of the survival of the fittest explained the astonishing ascent of life, the original question would remain unanswered: wherefrom the drive?[1]

No one has proved, as a general thesis, that it is the fittest who survive. There are a number of demonstrations, perhaps rather illustrations, of special cases; but, as a general proposition this mere hypothesis of the survival of the fittest does not seem to be scientifically proved at all. It is all very well to explain that the anteater survived because it 'developed' a long, sharp beak that allowed it to delve into ant-heaps and feed on ants. But no one has proved that in those days (which?) there was nothing to eat but ants; and, even if it were so, what did the anteater do

[1] 'Sir Peter said the main weakness of modern evolutionary theory was its lack of a fully worked out theory of variation—of candidature for evolution, of the forms in which genetic variants were proffered for selection. We had therefore no convincing account of evolutionary progress—of the otherwise inexplicable tendency of organisms to adopt ever more complicated solutions of the problems of remaining alive.' From a report in *The Times* (September 9, 1966) on an address by Sir Peter Medawar, F.R.S., director of the [British] National Institute for Medical Research, before the British Association for the Advancement of Science.

As fit comment to this forthright statement from an eminent biologist I give in an appendix quotations from R. L. Gregory, *Eye and Brain* (World University Library, Weidenfeld & Nicolson, London, W.1. and McGraw Hill Publishing Co., New York, 1967).

148

during the ages it needed to 'develop' its beak? And why, among the many animals that lived at the same time, was it the only one that bethought itself of—or was reduced to— growing such a weird protuberance?

If an objective study were attempted—and were possible— of 'survival', with or without 'natural selection', *as it really has happened* and free from any hypothesis to pre-explain it, the most likely conclusion as to the fitness of creatures that actually survived would be neutral: some fitter, others less fit, than those that were discarded. A situation does not seem ever to have arisen of so exacting a nature as to let some species pass and others fail, as in an entrance examination. Situations were always vague and wide, except in times of glacier formations or planetary catastrophes. But this second idea is not welcome to the many biologists who prefer to have a long quiet time for their evolutionary views to unroll themselves. Nowadays, thanks to Velikovsky, a different perspective begins to appear, one in which life is seen as a series of cycles of evolution broken by catastrophes—a view which, after all, was also that of Cuvier.

There are species that do not impress one as particularly gifted for survival and yet they do survive—worms, slugs, moles. Man himself, when his emergence on earth is better known, is not likely to impress anyone as having qualities fitting him for survival that would allow an observer– guesser to augur what his future was to be. As I write these lines, the press broadcasts the discovery of a type of man who is supposed to have dwelt in Africa about a couple of million years ago. His height was just over one meter (107 cms.). True, he had a human brain, seemingly; but is it being claimed that human intelligence is the outcome of a mutation or series of mutations aiming at ensuring the survival of a certain type of anthropoid? Then why have gorillas survived?

The explanation, therefore, fails because it is not proved

that natural selection be either necessary or sufficient for the 'survival' of the 'fittest', or that it is the fittest that always or even usually survive.

What really needs explaining is the astonishing ascent of life from the amoeba to the brain of a human genius. Who asserts that such an ascent had to be the inevitable outcome of natural selection? In the eyes of science, natural selection can be due only to pressure from the environment that eliminates the less fit, or to sheer chance. We have seen that the evidence before us does not warrant our acceptance of natural selection as a guide. Chance, given ages of time, can achieve wonders; yet it is hard to see how, within its own rule (which excludes all rules), it could achieve a continuously ascending evolution.[1]

Let me say again (for the third time) that we are not trying to explain a mere series of changes; but a series of transformations through centuries and centuries, presenting two remarkable features: an astonishing, constant ascent towards ever more complexity, freedom, initiative, and *a simultaneous survival of many, probably most, older types*. Both of these features must be briefly considered.

There is a manifest *orientation* of animal evolution, which reaches its summit in man. In the series of changes that make it up, four should be singled out: mobility, capacity to be aware of what goes on, self-awareness, and language. Life is already directed towards the last of these four revolutions from the time of the first one. It is a *directed evolution*. But even admitting that evolution in most other fields has been gentle enough to take place by means of unimportant mutations, there would still remain these three formidable leaps: from motionlessness to motion, from unawareness to

---

[1] True, this continuously ascending evolution may be, seems indeed to be, just a branch of the many-branched evolution; and then the chance of one of these branches developing in the ascending direction would appear as less aberrant. But this would just reduce, and only slightly, the extreme unlikelihood of the aberrance persisting in its ascending line.

awareness, and from self-ignorance to the dawn of the self. 'Evolution' does not possess enough vigour to power any of these three leaps.

If it were a mere matter of producing in each era the aptest being for it, the less apt beings and species might have been eliminated as useless failures or as obsolete forms. But the fact is that they *also* survive. The fittest survive along with the less fit, the new prototype and the old ones; and it happens that a whole species is born, grows, declines and dies out without other species, neither more nor less fit for the epoch, budging from their serene persistence. Evolution is then directed towards man, yet not exclusively so; for it advances along a wide front in a number of directions, most of which bear but little relation to the ultimate appearance of man. It might be likened to a tree of ideas rising in diverging directions as branches do, yet on the whole upwards (which does not entirely rule out this or that growth backwards or downwards, or a withered branch here and there); and among these branches there is one that shoots upwards and leads to man. Three features rule this phenomenon: the dynamic vigour of the whole, the freedom and width of the creative front, and the persistence of progress in, at any rate, certain types or branches.

None of these features would appear to find favour in the established version of evolution. For the establishment, evolution is automatic and blind. At the outset, a happy stroke of chance—of an ultra-astronomic unlikelihood capable of shattering all laws of the calculus of probabilities —produces the first heavy molecules. How the cell was born—we don't know. How mobility is *induced*—we don't know. And so, step after step, from blind fluke to blind fluke, until we reach Shakespeare's tragedies and the last quartets of Beethoven, every hour is a mystery for the man of science. For by virtue of a discipline that, far from diminishing, honours him, the man of science forbids himself the only explanation possible: a continuous creation by an ever free Creator.[1]

For us, however, who are neither subject to nor limited by such a discipline, the problem appears in a more favourable light. For us, observation is still a slave, but conclusion is free.

And observation does permit not a few conclusions. To begin with, life is a direct and undoubted manifestation of a superior intelligence. To return to a vocabulary more than once used in these pages, the goings on in creation are *deeds*, not facts. No chance, no natural selection could just at random build up the two optical cameras that man carries on either side of his nose and have placed them precisely there. 'Ah, but among blind animals the one with eyes survived'. To begin with, that is not the way it happened; and then, how did the blind ones guess that the luminous world existed? It does not make sense to deny that there was a provident, intelligent, creative agent who met the pheno-menon—light—with the apparatus—eyes.

---

[1] The most up-to-date version I know of the chemical origin of life is summed up in a Forum Service article (August 28, 1965) by Joseph G. Miller, which could itself be summed up as follows: 1. The original atmosphere of the earth was composed of water vapour, hydrogen, methane, and ammonia. 2. In 1952, Dr. Stanley Miller of the University of Chicago, by forcing methane, hydrogen, and ammonia past a high energy electrical spark, found in the resulting liquids, among other complex organic molecules, a few amino acids. 3. Sydney W. Fox's experiments (State University of Florida, 1957) proved that these amino acids might have become linked into more complex protein molecules. 4. As far back as 1924 the Russian scientist Oparin had already 'argued' that these molecules *might* have formed clusters that look very much like amoebas. *Et voilà pourquoi votre fille est muette.*

Cf. Dr. Dombrowski (article quoted): 'So that, within the laws of probability, a molecule of albumen with its twenty different aminoacids could emerge through mere chance and, what is more, conserve its structure throughout the hereditary process, no less than $10^{1270}$ (i.e. a 1 followed by 1,270 noughts) molecules would have to prove themselves unfit for it. Less ambitiously, such an initial molecule might be assumed to have been formed by a smaller number of animoacids. In all likelihood, it would not turn up as the outcome of the last trial after the rejection of many thousands of billions of unfit com-binations, for such a process would have required a longer time than the age of the universe. However, it is just as unlikely that this first construction fit for life could be a creation of mere chance.'

This agent conceived, elected, separated human light. For there is a human light as there is a dog light, a fly light, and a light for every species. Nature provides a scale of vibrations of such a kind that, transferred through the eyes to the human brain, they bring out the colours of the spectrum when their frequency is comprised within certain limits; but when their frequencies go beyond those of violet at one end and red at the other, they report darkness. These colours and this darkness are our luminous world. Our light, therefore, goes on in our brain when certain vibrations (of *what*, we do not know) enter through our eyes. A gift of seeing—and of hearing, and similarly for the other senses—has been granted to man; but it is strictly limited. There is therefore a purpose, a measure, a previous decision, an intelligence.

This intelligence does not follow, it precedes evolution since it precreates it and is ever immeasurably high above the beings that owe it their life. The intelligence implicit in the fly is immeasurably superior to that of the fly; and the intelligence implicit in the human brain is immeasurably superior to that which dwells in it and finds expression through it. Of all the strange aspects that the current scientific idea of evolution offers to the free observer (free from professional fetters) perhaps the strangest might be this sleight of hand whereby intelligence is made to vanish from nature, life, creation—whatever word you may choose to describe that which is the substance and *primum mobile* of evolution.

Consider this contrast. Biologists, paleontologists, anthropologists, agree in dating the dawn of *homo sapiens* at the day when man invents tools. But nature, does she invent eyes, ears, and other wonderful tools just at random, with neither intelligence nor purpose? Is not that attitude wondrously indifferent to logic? The fundamental fact about evolution is not its *how* but its *why*. Whence come its creative drive, its intention, its foresight? How can we disregard *abstract thought* in the homology of certain organs belonging to different species? Does not mimetism reveal a certain *unity of style* in Creation? There are caterpillars that look like stems, or stems that look like caterpillars. The circle, the cylinder, the star are designs that live both in the animal and in the vegetal kingdoms. There are infusoria which the microscope reveals as works of art worthy of a silver-smith specializing in filigree, other which make one think of vaults built by an architect. The symmetries of flowers and crystals harmonize with the geometry invented by man's brain.

Intelligence is thus the first gift which manifests itself in the creatures, but another free and less foreseeable gift soon reveals itself in nature. Mere intelligence makes means and ends fit, instruments and functions tally; therefore it tends towards economy and utility. But in creation, what strikes the observer, what indeed astounds him, is the profusion, the imagination, the fantasy. Economy does not seem to prevail. There is, of course, economy in nature, as there is everything; but what prevails is waste. It seems that one masculine ejection would be enough to fertilize all the women of the earth. Think of that masterpiece, the flower, and how millions and millions of them blow and die even in spots where no one will ever enjoy their beauty—unless it be their Creator; and as for their aroma, so that the young girl of the house may enjoy the scent of one of her roses for a few seconds every few days, all the roses of her garden flood the air with their perfume twenty-four hours a day. Nature gives herself without stint.

What a strange aberration misleads so many first-rate minds into interpreting evolution in rationalistic and utilitarian terms? Would it not be more reasonable, if less rationalistic, to see it as the ever-alive shooting forth of spontaneous new creations emanating from a fecund spirit unable to repress his creative force, as we know happens with every true artist? He must create. How could he help it?

154

This is the dominant impression left on anyone who visits a garden in the spring, or beholds an aquarium animated with unbelievable shapes, or a bird sanctuary swarming with lively wings.

Nor is the world a miracle of mere imagination. There is fantasy as well in it. Imagination that creates new forms within the system, inventing, for instance: reptiles, birds, quadrupeds, men; fantasy to throw in as well birds, reptiles, and mammals that, made for land, prefer to live in the water; talking birds; forms and colours of an extravagant variety; jokes and games as closely connected with Darwin and Wallace as Carnival is with Lent.

And this freedom and even licence which Creation reveals is so boundless that, following this path, it seems as if the Creator might in the end vanish into a mere form of Hazard —were it not that Hazard does not create. Furthermore, it so happens—and this is a point to think on—that along with all this feast and carnival of fantasies, Creation persistently maintains a steady line of progress or ascensions from the first molecule of protein and the first cell to man's brain and its works; therefore, a will and an initiative that knows where it is going.

Science sees evolution in a rationalistic and utilitarian light, and yet neither directed in itself nor determined by any economic sense of things. Science, therefore, sees evolution as rational and utilitarian in its effects but not in its causes. Moreover, it observes the data provided by the general biology of evolution as a whole, and endeavours to explain the changes that occur by observing and comparing bones with bones, organs with organs, and functions with functions.

There is another way of broaching the problem, one more attentive to the why than to the how of evolution. It consists in trying to collect as many hints as possible that are likely to throw light on the nature of the original impulse that drives evolution. Just as in day to day life we can gradually form an opinion on what kind of a person our neighbour is by repeated observations of his ways and actions, so we may gradually form an idea of this initial impulse by observing how species, forms of life, types, and characters appear, develop, and disappear throughout the history of evolution. What do we expect to find—a person, a machine, an abstract idea? None of these preconceived shapes, offered to us by our limited imagination, will fit the great reality hidden behind the data, but which the data, if well observed, may reveal to us—at least in its essence.

Perhaps the most significant of these observations might be the one that we made at the beginning of the first stage of our journey: the Creator imagines first a vertical kingdom, that of vegetal life; then, goes through ages of an animal kingdom, which is horizontal, before crowning it all with a vertical species far more developed than anything that had come before. It seems that in this pattern of events we are witnessing a revelation or adumbration of ulterior plans: that in the divine imagination man was already alive when the business-in-hand was only the creation of speechless and motionless plants.

This surmise takes on body and vigour when we observe the astonishing parallelism between the body of the tree and the spirit of man. The Creator shapes the tree so that it already prefigures the human creature actually to emerge millions of years later. Is not this likeness between tree and man across the ages a more significant feature of Creation than any relation between or among teeth, tibias, or skulls? Can a clearer assertion be imagined of an intent to create man at the end of evolution than this creation, at its beginning, of the tree with all there is of 'human' in it?

Let us now recall how entranced we were by the trees that *gesticulate though motionless*. This means that ages before the Creator gave life to man He took pleasure in shedding on his dawning Creation glimmers of what His ultimate creature would be, sculpting into the tree gestures not yet

156

born, just as Beethoven, in the scherzo of the Ninth Symphony, drops hints of the great final theme.

It seems as if already, from the first movement of His Life–Symphony, the Creator had felt the human theme singing in His inner self; and so He lets it come through now and then in what He does. On my visits to New York I never fail to repair to the zoo in Central Park mainly to call on a buffalo (or rather bison), earnest and bearded, and so human that he always reminds me of a number of acquaintances. While I behold him, I cannot help feeling or fearing that he is going to treat me to a harangue on the rights of man, or on the progress of surgery, or on some one or another of the subjects that bearded men are fond of holding forth about, in words shaped with pipe-smoke. 'Is it possible', I wonder, outwardly impassive and silent so that the good man, I mean bison, does not guess my thoughts—'is it possible that when He imagined this creature the Creator was not thinking of pulling the leg of some radical-socialist?'

Evolution does seem to be teeming with anticipations, glimmers, hints of what man will be, fleeting illuminations that leave us wondering. That squirrel, which has got hold of a nut at the feet of the cow and run away to eat it behind the tree, and is now sitting on the grass cracking the husk with its teeth and extracting the kernel with its nails, how human it is already in its gestures, in its vivacity, its intelligent attention to everything that goes on around. And here again we are fascinated to observe how in every animal, and even in every vegetal species, there seems to live some kind of premonition of the human character—the fiery, the cowardly, the gay, the melancholy, the 'brooding' (borrowed from the birds), the flighty, and the 'hare'-brained; so that it all looks very much as if the Creator had been trying His hand at creating human characters while He gave forth roses and carnations, tigers and hares, sharks and snails.

157

How welcome, how apt here that gambolling of fantasy, that flying off at a tangent, that irresponsible joking which can be seen everywhere springing up unexpectedly in nature! We had occasion to meditate on this wonderful mystery when watching the marvellous parrot. Who, by the way, poses a problem bordering on an enigma. The parrot and his close cousins, such as the cockatoo, reveal an obvious aptitude to shape words and phrases borrowed from human speech. We assume that they are even less aware of what they are saying than many human beings; but as musical instruments, if the image is acceptable, their gizzards must be comparable to the human throat. Therefore, in Creation, the physical capacity to produce human speech turns up long before speech itself.

Once again, we catch the Creator in His intimate laboratory imagining what later shall be, adumbrating germs of future ideas, preparing the ground for ulterior inventions. He seems to have already had human speech in mind when He invented the parrot, whom He endows with a larynx and vocal chords that will enable him *eventually* to speak. But if we consider speech not merely as a system of sounds but as a medium for communication, rudiments of language emerge freely enough here and there in Creation. Bees convey information on good pastures by means of dances and movements orientated on carefully chosen axes. Birds may sing more often than not *ex abundantia cordis* (who would not sing if he could fly?), yet probably also at times with a definite intent. Hens, according to several studies, seem to dispose of up to three dozen conventional sounds amounting to a rudimentary language.[1] And similar claims are made for chimpanzees and gorillas. Here, then, as in other cases, we can witness the gradual

[1] Not to speak of human interpretations of what they say, sometimes so forcefully. One of these, current in Chile, puts the following words to the hen's music while laying an egg: 'All this happens to me [*bis*]—Because I have no character [*bis*].'

growth of an idea that in the course of ages will flourish into a human feature.

Habits, the 'mores' of animals, would appear to adjust to the same pattern of growth and evolution towards the human. Is is not wonderful that long before man appears in Creation monogamy is the rule with some creatures, such as the parrot, and polygamy the rule with others, such as the bull? It looks as if the Creator had thought it wise to give a trial to the two systems before coming to man. It also looks as if His trials had not led Him to a definite conclusion. One is drawn to similar reflections when observing the experiments made by the Creator with ants, bees, and termites before launching forth (with an admirable optimism, it would appear) to create human societies.

All this seems to favour the view that the idea of man grows apace with the aeons in the Creator's imagination. Now and then one or other of the organs, faculties, powers of the future being turns up in a present creation at the time—the tree, the squirrel, the bee, the parrot—and the idea goes on accumulating its characteristic components throughout the ages, just as if the Creator Who manifests Himself in the creation or pre-evolution of all these things were above all an artist. Nor is it without significance that artistic invention is known among men as *creation*.

We might perhaps dare now suggest a bold correction to the idea of evolution as understood by most biologists. Yes. There is an evolution, but not *horizontal*, not a passing of one set of forms onto another set of forms in the course of time; but *vertical*, the new set of forms emerging suddenly in nature from the mind of the Creator, and therefore without an inevitable subjection to the environment. Not, however, either by caprice or by sheer hazard. Evolution would essentially be the variation of the creative thought which gives forth forms after forms, bearing in mind the preceding ones and yet not altogether dependent on them; a variation knowing where it goes, yet free and capable of creating natural fantasies and carnivals just for the fun of it, out of a sheer exuberance of imagination and power.

If this view were accepted, the official attitude towards evolution would have to be understood as the outcome of the persistence of the cow; a bias in favour of the horizontal tradition that insists on seeing life as a herd of facts, a river of cow-loins flowing down the valley of time; while the observation of all that does not fit in with this horizontal view of evolution leads us to the image of a vertical Creator in Whose mind an evolution of ideas and forms takes place that He will eventually manifest in nature, not in a horizontal line or by material derivation of previously created forms, but in vertical springs surging from the river bed as mutations or new inventions—though, of course, in relation to the old.

What does it matter?, it might be asked. Perhaps a good deal. From the moment that man appears, the Creator shares His Creation with His creature. If Creation is vertical, as seems evident, it does matter that man should keep to a tree rather than a cow attitude, a *what* and a *why* rather than a *how* attitude, the feeling of innovation rather than that of mere derivation or change. From the day man appears, the deeds of the Lord tend more and more to be achieved by and through man. The astounding command over nature that man has been achieving at a growing pace during the last century—a prelude, it would seem, to even more astonishing conquests—augurs a prodigious future for the human being.

But we must bow to the facts. This future will not blossom unless quality is saved from quantity, the tree from the cow. Too many signs in modern society point to a rebellion of quantity against quality, as Ortega in his day masterfully pointed out. Whole societies are already living under the sway of quantity; the interstellar successes of the Soviet Union should not blind us to this sad fact. The future of man depends on the future of freedom, so that the stems of higher inherent stature may, without hindrance, reach their natural size.

So to the numerous reasons in support of liberty, one must be added which might well be the deepest and the most pregnant with significance. Let man be free as the instrument of the Creator. Through him, if he can and dares unite intelligence, initiative and creative capacity, the Spirit will work. And let us not be impressed by the lowing of the quantitative cows at this clear word—Spirit—the supreme symbol of quality and of vertical impetus.

The idea or archetype here described as the Creator prejudges nothing as to His essence outside what we have already noted while observing life and evolution: intelligence, initiative, fecundity in esthetic creation—powers that recall the human faculties of the same name, but of course immeasurably higher. For the rest, the spirit of man, while the cow grazes at his feet, will go on for centuries of centuries rising, stretching his arms like tree branches, longing and yearning at least to touch with the tips of his fingers, the buds of its twigs, the blue veil that conceals the mystery.

# APPENDIX[1]

The problem of how eyes have developed has presented a major challenge to the Darwinian theory of evolution by Natural Selection. We can make many entirely useless experimental models when designing a new instrument, but this was impossible for Natural Selection, for each step must confer some advantage upon its owner, to be selected and transmitted through the generations. But what use is a half-made lens? What use is a lens giving an image, if there is no nervous system to interpret the information. How could a visual nervous system come about before there was an eye to give it information? In evolution there can be no master plan, no looking ahead to form structures which, though useless now, will come to have importance when other structures are sufficiently developed. And yet the human eye and brain have come about through slow painful trial and error.[2] [p. 25.]

We are concerned in this book with human eyes, and how we see the world. Our eyes are typical vertebrate eyes, and are not among the most complex or highly developed, though the human brain is the most elaborate of all brains. Complicated eyes often go with simple brains—we find eyes of incredible complexity in pre-vertebrates serving tiny brains. The compound eyes of arthropods (including insects) consist not of a single lens with a retina of many thousands or millions of receptors, but rather of many lenses with but a single receptor element for each lens. The earliest known fossil eye belongs to the Trilobites—which lived over 500,000,000 years ago—the earliest preserved fossils being

---

[1] From *Eye and Brain*, by R. L. Gregory. [See footnote on p. 148].

[2] May I point out that this conclusion does not tally with what precedes. It is dogmatic, not scientific, *in spite*, not *because*, of what goes before. Moreover, when the author says 'has presented' he suggests that the challenge has been victoriously answered; actually, however, it has not been.

found in Cambrian rocks. In many species of trilobite, the eyes were highly developed. The external structure of these most ancient eyes may be seen perfectly preserved. . . . We can see nothing now of the internal structure, only the outer form is tantalizingly with us now. They were compound eyes, rather like those of a modern insect: some had over a thousand facets. [p. 27.]

Among the most curious eyes in the whole of nature is that of a creature the size of a pin's head—a little known copepod—COPILLA. She (the males are dull by comparison) has a pair of image-forming eyes, which function neither like vertebrate nor like compound eyes, but something like a television camera. One would give a lot to know why it exists, and whether it is the remaining example of a very early kind of eye. If COPILLA is an evolutionary failure she deserves a prize for originality. [pp. 28–29.]

# INDEX

166

167